Making a Small Garden

A Wisley Gardening Companion

Making a Small Garden

GEOFFREY K. COOMBS
and
KEITH RUSHFORTH

Cassell

The Royal Horticultural Society

THE ROYAL HORTICULTURAL SOCIETY

Cassell Educational Limited
Villiers House, 41/47 Strand
London WC2N 5JE
for the Royal Horticultural Society

First published 1993

British Library Cataloguing in Publication Data
A catalogue record for this book is available from the
British Library

ISBN 0–304–32042–0

Photographs by Eric Crichton, Andrew Lawson,
Photos Horticultural, Paul Roberts, Keith Rushforth,
Harry Smith Collection
Plans by Geoffrey K. Coombs

Phototypesetting by RGM Associates, Southport
Printed in Hong Kong by Wing King Tong Co. Ltd.

Page 2: Shade is a common problem in small gardens, but may
be overcome with the right choice of plants (see p. 75)

Contents

In a secluded corner roses overhang a garden seat and pots of summer
flowering plants, herbs and strawberries stand nearby

Foreword

The first Wisley Handbooks, published in 1972, launched this most successful series, which has sold more than a million copies to date. From the beginning they have identified the subjects of most interest to the gardener. They originated as articles and lectures delivered to the Royal Horticultural Society, reprinted from the RHS *Journal*. One of the first pamphlets, *Hardy and Semi-Hardy Annuals in the Open Air*, sold for 2d. in 1915. Many of these early leaflets advised gardeners on wartime needs.

With the support and involvement of RHS staff as well as many other excellent authors, the Handbooks have always given clear and concise practical advice, ensuring their success. The first Handbooks were 24 pages, stapled, with black and white illustrations. Now there are more than 60 Handbooks, each of 64 pages and illustrated in colour.

This volume, *Making a Small Garden*, brings together four of the Handbooks, *Plans for Small Gardens*, *Plans for Small Gardens 2*, *Shrubs for Small Gardens* and *Trees for Small Gardens*. It provides, in a concise and readily available form, valuable information on garden planning and planting and is an ideal reference work.

A pleasing and enjoyable garden can be created from the most unpromising of sites. The key is the planning – and your enthusiasm. Here, 35 garden plans, with lists of suitable plants, provide a starting point. You may be aiming for a family garden, a plantsman's garden or one that incorporates fruit and vegetables. Others may want to create a scented garden, or to learn how to use the available space most effectively, to produce attractive plant associations or to fit a glasshouse into the design unobtrusively. All of these points are included, even the making of a garden within a garden, such as a herb or heather garden. By careful planning, even the most problematical site may be transformed into a garden of charm and character to provide all the year round pleasure for all the family.

The aims of the early Handbooks, to interest and inform gardeners, are amply fulfilled in this most helpful compilation.

Christopher Brickell,
Director General,
The Royal Horticultural Society

9

Plans for
Small Gardens

— GEOFFREY K. COOMBS —

The boundary fences of this small garden are well hidden by
plants. Clematis and alpine plants thrive in the limy soil

Introduction

It is wishful thinking to suppose that in a book of garden plans a design can be found to fit exactly into one's own plot and fulfil all the requirements of a new garden, or perhaps meet the needs and revised ideas for one long established. It is, however, likely that certain sections and features can be usefully applied from a ready-made plan or parts of several plans, such as arrangements for grouping shrubs and plants having regard for colour and spacing for specific purposes and places. The shape of a terrace for example could be taken in part from one plan and perhaps the outline of a border from another. Suggestions will be found for siting a greenhouse, garden shed and vegetables, all of which are common ingredients of many gardens differing in size and shape.

Opposite: A sink garden is a good way to grow small, choice plants
Below: Steps can be planted with fragrant plants

It is probably safe to say that many successful garden layouts, both on a grand scale and the smallest plot, started to take shape on a drawing board. The advantage of applying ideas to paper are manifold; one is that the whole area can be seen from a birds-eye view and gives a better idea of proportions. Another advantage is that different shapes of beds can be drawn and easily changed, paths put in position and eliminated at will, or the design of a terrace that appears to be wrong quickly erased.

I think that designing a garden is reminiscent of browsing through the glorious displays of a new seed catalogue in January, seemingly bringing the splendour of summer a little nearer. The similarity lies in the fact that when one begins the design the most uncompromising plot may be revealed as the garden of our dreams.

The basic essentials at this early stage are a measuring tape at least 60ft (18m) in length, a metal spike to secure the end (in lieu of someone to hold it) and a large writing pad. In addition wooden pegs, a straight edge, and spirit level are needed to establish levels; for larger areas boning rods may be required. These are T-shaped and consist of an upright leg about 4ft (1.2m) long and a cross member about 18 inches (45cm) long set at right angles at the top. A sighting is made by checking that the tops of the horizontal bar are in line.

It is worth spending a little time measuring as accurately as possible because one finishes with a plan that is to scale and recognizably similar in outline to the garden. The plan may be used to design beds in a specific shape and size, and to mark the position of other items in the design.

The drawing opposite illustrates a few principles for measuring a small area of land.

It is unusual for a plot to be exactly rectangular and the position of the house is not always parallel to the boundaries. By using the sides of the house as the datum and measuring by triangulation, the positions of the boundaries are established together with permanent features that have to be considered and eventually incorporated into the garden.

With regard to design I always follow the maxim that if it looks right on paper it will work out to a satisfactory conclusion on the ground. The drawing opposite shows how a shape can be accurately transferred to the site by using a boundary as a datum line and from this measurements are made at right angles at selected intervals to establish a curved outline.

Something should be said about 'shape' with reference to plant material. The outline of the borders and variations in heights produced by carefully placed specimen trees and shrubs at

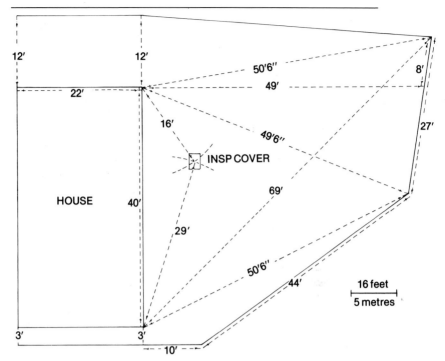

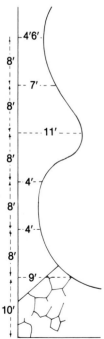

Above: How to measure a small area of land: the sides of the house are taken as a base for accurately measuring the boundaries and position of features on the site.

Left: Transferring a shape from the plan to the site: by using the boundary as a datum line measurements can be made at right angles at selected intervals to establish a curved outline.

Opposite: The enthusiast's garden at Wisley, one of a series of model gardens designed to show the potential of small plots
Above: *Geranium endressii*, an attractive and useful ground cover plant for a position in light shade (see p.18)

certain places will constitute the framework for a design; an example of this, as a detail, is illustrated under 'Narrow gardens' (p.41) by the simple shaping of a border and placing a narrow columnar tree towards the apex of the widest part of the bed which gives emphasis to a focal point.

Spacing is a vital technique. Shrubs and trees must be given enough space to grow, otherwise the plants will become over-crowded and shapeless. By advance planning, i.e. drawing the planting plan on paper to scale and allowing enough space for development, this situation can be avoided. When the plant first arrives it is difficult to appreciate that a shrub only 2 feet (60cm) high could increase to three times its size in three years. A nursery catalogue that gives the height, spread and flowering time to-gether with other information about plants will give a good idea of allowances to be made. For example if the total width of a phil-adelphus is 10 feet (3m), the space around the plant should have a radius of 5 feet. If the shrubs next to it in the bed will grow to 8 feet (2.5m) wide, the plants should be positioned 9 feet (2.7m) apart. This is of course a long-term solution, and by allowing enough room there is much bare ground round the newly planted shrubs.

There are several ways of bridging the interim period between planting and growing. The ideal way of making a garden look established from the beginning is in the use of ground cover plants. In the bare ground between the shrubs plant drifts and groups of carpeters that will make a complete ground cover without competing with the larger plants. The specimen shrubs may also be shown to better advantage by the plants underneath if carefully chosen for colour of flowers and foliage (an example of this is the scarlet-flowered *Rhododendron* 'Britannia' and *Saxifraga umbrosa*, the foam-like pink flowers of the latter combining well with the stronger tone of the rhododendron and the glossy green rosette of leaves making a dense carpet on the ground). Other easily propagated carpeters and therefore expendable are *Polygonum affine* 'Darjeeling Red' and 'Donald Lowndes' (see p. 47), *Stachys* 'Silver Carpet', *Geranium endressii* (see p. 17) and several cultivars of *Campanula*. Some of the plants that have been used primarily to cover the ground will be suppressed by the shrubs as they spread outwards but they will have made a most useful contribution to the border and in the open places some will remain and continue to grow.

Some shrubs make a much more significant feature if several of the same are planted close together in order to make one bold unit, for example *Ceratostigma willmottianum*, the small-growing shrub roses and hardy fuchsias. Depending on the size of the border many others can be planted in groups of three or more, the distances between the plants in a triangle being 18 inches to 2 feet apart (45 to 60cm) so that they join together making one substantial unit 6 feet across (1.8m) in a shorter time than if only one is planted. This practice can be adopted throughout the planting scheme and in large beds shrubs such as *Cotoneaster salicifolius rugosus* could be 3 feet apart (60–90cm) but allowing 8 to 10 feet (2.6–3.1m) on the outer sides for development.

Most shrubs benefit from judicious pruning at some time, if only to nip back a wayward branch to maintain a good shape; for many others regular pruning is essential to obtain good results and has some bearing on spacing because, although in theory if a shrub is allowed to grow naturally it will attain a certain height and spread, its size can be contained by annual and careful pruning.

A typical example is *Buddleja davidii* cultivars which will eventually attain 10 to 15 feet (3–4.5m) with a gaunt open structure of branches, but by pruning hard in March a well shaped shrub within the space of 6 feet (1.8m) is maintained. Other shrubs that do not normally need hard pruning can also be contained within a smaller space than natural growth demands. It sometimes happens that with certain conifers and very large shrubs the spread of the lower branches exceeds the allotted space with the result that a view is hidden or access is obstructed. In some circumstances such conifers can be saved from destruction by removing the lower lateral branches up to 6 to 7 ft (2–2.25m) from the ground to leave a clean stem as shown below. If there are two or three main stems the branches can be removed in the same way making the tree in the shape of a standard with multiple stems. Shrubs that attain tree-like proportions respond equally well to similar pruning. The shrubby magnolias (see p. 20) are usually low branched in earlier years but eventually attain a height of up to 25 ft (7.5m), and if several of the largest ascending branches are selected and all other lower growth removed it is sometimes possible to have what is in effect a small tree in a limited space. The bay *(Laurus nobilis)* and *Genista aetnensis,* and in mild districts, *Pittosporum* are other examples of shrubs that can be treated in this way.

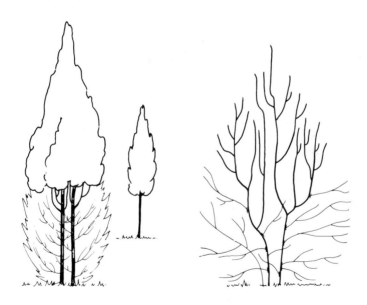

Access near a path or drive may be improved by the removal of lower branches from conifers and large shrubs

Above: The magnolias provide a useful range for the small garden. There are many different species and hybrids available, especially forms of *Magnolia × soulangiana* which is one of the most popular. Illustrated here is *Magnolia × soulangiana* 'Rustic Rubra'

Opposite: The 'family' garden – one of the model gardens at Wisley. This garden has been adapted from the plan on page 27, but the essential features remain the same

Whether starting with a bare site or changing an existing garden, the order of work should be based on a definite programme. This will include clearing, levelling and drainage and, if it involves moving heavy material, should be completed before more delicate operations such as laying the lawn are carried out. It is sensible to construct paths and paved areas at an early stage to improve access and, when it comes to making the lawn, this can be raised slightly above the paving, which facilitates mowing.

If sowing a lawn, it is a good idea to place a single line of turf

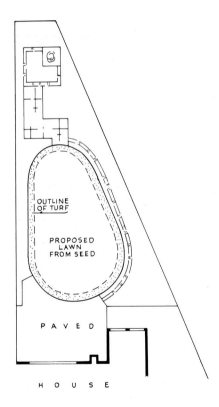

OUTLINE
OF TURF

PROPOSED
LAWN
FROM SEED

P A V E D

H O U S E

A line of turf round the perimeter of a newly sown lawn gives a firm edge immediately

Elaeagnus pungens 'Maculata' makes a fine evergreen hedge, particularly when interspersed with clematis and climbing roses

round the entire perimeter of the area (see opposite). This is particularly useful on light sandy soil where the edges of the lawn may be slow to consolidate. It gives a very satisfactory immediate outline, so that the garden looks as if it is taking shape, and within a few days allows one to cut a firm neat edge round the newly sown lawn. It is more economical to divide each piece of turf lengthwise in half, which is still wide enough for the purpose.

Hedges or other screens, flower beds and paths are three of the most important basic items in a design. Hedges used for division (as opposed to boundary hedges) help to give structure to a garden, although the expense of planting them is sometimes begrudged. They provide a background for the plants in front of them, just as walls enclose and complement the decor of a room. An evergreen hedge which might be thought sombre and dull can be interspersed with sections of square trellis of the same height and roses or shrubs can be trained against it to introduce colour (see overleaf).

Hedges sometimes create competitive root problems. Privet is a notorious offender and the roots spread over a wide area, particularly when close to a bed that has been dug and manured. Fortunately, many of the old privet hedges which were so common in front and back gardens have been replaced. However,

23

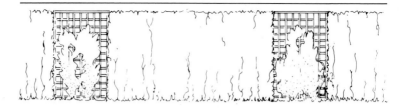

A hedge line broken with sections of trellis against which shrubs or roses can be trained

those that remain can be controlled by digging a narrow trench to a depth of about 2 feet (60 cm), 1 to $1\frac{1}{2}$ feet (30–45 cm) away from the base, and burying pieces of old plastic or corrugated iron (often obtainable as scrap from a builder). These should be placed level with or just below the ground and will be completely hidden when the trench is filled in (see below). Lilac, a close relative of privet, and other invasive shrubs which impoverish the soil around them, can be treated in a similar way. The trench should enable the bed to be manured without the widespreading shrubs receiving most of the benefit.

Paths and paved areas open up many variations in design and, with old material put to new use, concrete is now an ingredient in many products. Concrete bricks and small slabs (known as setts) lend themselves to sweeping fluid curves and circles around features such as a modern sculpture or urn. Paving stones or concrete can be laid in squares, say 3 feet (90cm) wide, and the squares edged with grey or reddish bricks, which combine well with the colours, to make an interesting pattern and texture.

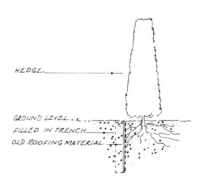

Above: Old roofing material buried to prevent roots spreading
Opposite: A new garden with a bed of dwarf conifers and heathers

A Family Garden

It could be said that the garden is a place of common interests, but diverse requirements, and sometimes the different needs are so many that it may seem impossible to include them all within a small space. There is, however, usually a common theme in the necessity to produce an attractive and colourful garden that is easily maintained, the latter being particularly necessary with a growing family which is inclined to make demands on free time at weekends.

The principal ingredients for a labour-saving garden are in many respects the same as those for any garden, consisting of flowering and evergreen shrubs, roses of all types and carpeting plants. But different age groups see the garden in different ways and those interested in climbing frames and swings for example will have little regard for the quality of the turf.

A sand-pit is often demanded by the youngest members of the family, and sometimes a place has to be found for a wendy house preferably in a sunny pleasant part of the garden and made a feature that is complementary to the whole design. Such a building has a relatively short life and it should be so arranged that after its removal the space can be planted and integrated with the rest of the garden.

Another feature is the children's garden where they can grow their own seeds and plants. This plot should occupy a favourable aspect and be likely to produce good results with little attention, otherwise the gardeners will be quickly discouraged. In plan 1 the children's garden is shown with a continuous border 4 feet wide (1.2 m) and bordered with a paved path. This could be divided into smaller areas by paving at right angles to the main path to make beds 4 feet square (1.2 m²) which would be easier to maintain and different crops could be grown separately. It will be seen that the layout gives a good space for lawn and there is a dry hard surface from the house leading to the wendy house, sand-pit and vegetable garden. The borders of mixed shrubs and plants will give colour and interest at different times of the year, but bear in mind when making the choice that the young cricketer will sometimes score a boundary, and the goal-keeper will occasionally let a ball through right into the centre of a flower-bed. At this stage in the garden's development it may be better to plant tougher shrubs and plants in preference to the rare and

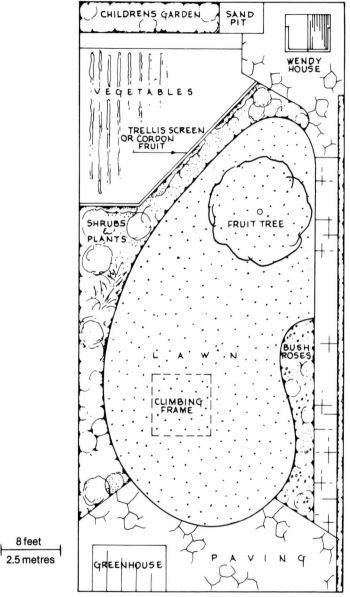

CHILDRENS GARDEN   SAND PIT

WENDY HOUSE

VEGETABLES

TRELLIS SCREEN
OR CORDON
FRUIT

SHRUBS
&
PLANTS

FRUIT TREE

LAWN

BUSH
ROSES

CLIMBING
FRAME

8 feet
2.5 metres

GREENHOUSE   PAVING

Plan 1: A design for a small garden incorporating some of the needs of a young family

delicate. Roses can stand quite a lot of punishment from breaking; even pruning down into the old wood sometimes produces new growth from parts that have been dormant for some years.

Basically the design is very simple, the primary object being to provide a lawn that extends throughout nearly the whole length and breadth of the garden by introducing diagonal lines to the borders; it also provides space for shrubs and flowers. The screen which divides the vegetable section could be replaced with cordon fruit trees instead of lattice and ornamental climbers.

Concern is sometimes expressed (and not without reason) about poisonous seeds and berries and the injuries produced by some garden plants; the following list contains trees and shrubs that are commonly found in gardens. They should be treated with discretion but whether they are all eliminated from the garden is a personal decision. Berries and seeds to which children might be particularly attracted are marked thus*.

	Aconitum napellus	monkshood
	Aquilegia	columbine
	Buxus	box
*	*Convallaria*	lily-of-the-valley
*	*Cotoneaster*	
*	*Crataegus*	hawthorn
*	*Daphne mezereum*	mezereon
	Delphinium	
	Digitalis	foxglove
*	*Euonymus*	
	europaeus	spindletree
	Fritillaria meleagris	snakeshead fritillary
	Hedera	ivy
	Helleborus	Christmas rose
*	*Ilex*	holly
	Laburnum	
*	*Lupinus*	
	Narcissus	daffodil
	Papaver	poppy
*	*Prunus*	
	laurocerasus	laurel
*	*Sorbus*	rowan

Some trees and shrubs repel touch with an armour of needle-sharp thorns; to mention only a few, most of the *Berberis*, *Yucca gloriosa* (Adam's needle) and some of the *Pyracantha*, are examples. *Robinia pseudoacacia* (false acacia) has a habit of dropping pieces of dead branch that bristle with large thorns, and *Hippophaë rhamnoides* (sea buckthorn), grown for its very attractive orange berries, has sharp spines.

Above: Monkshoods, in this case *Aconitum ferox*, have poisonous roots
Below: The aptly named silver hedgehog holly, *Ilex aquifolium* 'Ferox Argentea'

A Plantsman's Garden

The size of a garden has little to do with its quality and it is probably easier to maintain conditions of good cultivation in a very small garden than in a larger one.

The design in plan 2 is the layout of a very small garden for someone who wants to grow a wide range of plants that need almost as wide a range of differing environments and includes raised beds, a pool, a greenhouse, a scree garden, climbing plants and shrubs. In this instance the raised beds are no more than 18 ins (45cm) in height and would therefore be little higher than some sink gardens. Good drainage is essential and preparation of the beds should be thoroughly carried out at the beginning. (For preparing raised beds see the Wisley Handbook, *Alpines the Easy Way*.) It is intended that one of these areas is given over to rock plants and one or two miniature shrubs and conifers.

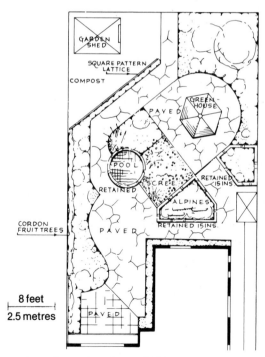

Plan 2: A connoisseur's garden, for varied interests

A sketch of the plan shown opposite

The flat bed next to the pool is covered with shingle over which plants can scramble; the roots are established in the soil beneath and the stones drawn up close around the stems. The planting is not intended to cover the scree completely, and the colour of the stones should be appropriate to complement the plants and provide an interesting feature in contrast to the paving. The other bed near the pool is also at ground level and is suitable for small shrubs and low perennial plants. The pool is also raised to the same height as the retained beds and the coping around the edge offers a place to sit and watch activity in the water. In a small pool however the choice has to be made between plants and fish or a fountain because the turbulent movement of the water will not be welcome to either. I think it is better to have a fountain with a low projector for a small garden and it is worth while looking carefully at the different types on the market. There is for instance the fountain where the water emerges from the top of a tube as a thin descending veil shaped like a shining dome or a bubble fountain when a jet just breaks the water from under the surface. Without any fish or plants the water can be kept clean and even a little blue by the addition of copper sulphate.

31

Above: *Chamaecyparis pisifera* 'Boulevard', deservedly one of the most popular dwarf conifers
Below: *Lithodora diffusa* 'Heavenly Blue' is a charming rock plant

Hydrangea petiolaris is ideal for covering a wall (see plan 3)

Another raised bed offers a place for plants that will not thrive in the natural soil of the garden, for instance adding peaty, lime-free compost for dwarf azaleas or light gritty conditions for plants that will not thrive in clay soil.

The greenhouse is functional but also an architectural feature in any garden and ideal in a place where the more conventional shape cannot be partially hidden.

The cordon fruit trees (see also p.52) represent a collection of pears and apples and if the fences or walls along the boundaries are not suitable for more fruit the lattice screen is ideal for a fan trained plum. Alternatively soft fruit such as redcurrants and gooseberries could be trained as cordons against a trellis, including several different cultivars in a small space. The quality of the fruit grown in this way is generally superior to that produced in the usual way on bushes.

Plan 3 includes many features that the interested gardener might like to include and although the plot slopes up from the house the design could equally well be applied to one that is flat. The principal means of access to the garden is by the central steps which are wide enough to give a spacious and unrestricted feeling on approaching the lawn. A paved terrace at the highest part of the garden is reached by three steps of generous proportions and adjacent to this a rock garden is appropriately sited on ground

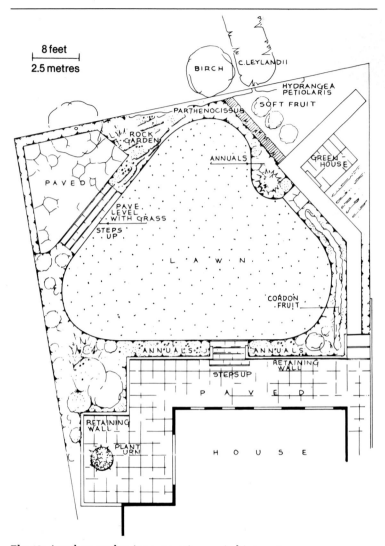

8 feet
2.5 metres

C.LEYLANDII
BIRCH
HYDRANGEA
PETIOLARIS
SOFT FRUIT
PARTHENOCISSUS
ROCK
GARDEN
ANNUALS
GREEN-
HOUSE
PAVED
PAVE
LEVEL
WITH GRASS
STEPS
UP
L A W N
CORDON
FRUIT
ANNUALS
ANNUALS
RETAINING
WALL
STEPS UP
P A V E D
RETAINING
WALL
PLANT
URN
H O U S E

Plan 3: Another garden incorporating varied interests

that is a natural slope.

In the opposite corner screened, by a low hedge of *Pyracantha* 'Watereri' there is a small area for soft fruit and salad crops and a greenhouse is sited with direct approach by a path from the house. The outline of the greenhouse is broken by a narrow conifer and cordon fruit trees that flank the path.

Opposite: Lady's mantle, *Alchemilla mollis*, a beautiful perennial for the front of a bed (see p. 36)

The charm of a garden may be its seclusion, and in a very small space this is not always easily achieved. In a large garden a grass walk may lead to a hidden arbour or small lawn separated from the main part of the garden by a screen of shrubs. Plan 4 (opposite) shows a very narrow plot 19 feet wide (5.5m) that has been divided into two sections. The one nearest the house with a lawn is the largest and the other is hidden from view by hedges planted at right angles from the boundaries.

Having regard for the width of the garden, the height of the hedges would be the best set at about 4 to 5 feet (1.5m). Choosing a plant that can be trimmed close and compact is preferable to a hedge that is happier at twice the height. *Pyracantha* 'Watereri' is ideal and responds well to cutting, and *Cotoneaster lacteus* is equally good.

English yew (*Taxus baccata*) gives a look of excellence to a garden and forms a superb hedge particularly on chalky soil, but prefers not to be restricted below 4 ft (1.2m). For further information see the Wisley Handbook *Hedges and Screens* by Mike Pollock. Two important features about the design are the figure in the middle garden which gives a point of interest at the end of the path and is seen from the house and terrace, and the sundial, in the same section, which is visible from the paving in front of the summerhouse. Both objects are included to create focal points from two directions apart from an architectural function in the centre section.

The larger border that flanks the lawn could be planted with medium and small sized shrubs interplanted with two or three groups of floribunda roses. The narrow bed on the right side of the paved path might accommodate plants that like to sprawl such as *Gypsophila* 'Pink Star', *Nepeta × faassenii*, *Campanula poscharskyana*, *Alchemilla mollis* (see p. 35) and a few more upright ones such as *Lavandula spica* 'Hidcote', *Agapanthus* (see p.48) and *Cheiranthus cherii* 'Harpur Crewe'.

If, in the middle garden, the statue is raised upon a small plinth, the surrounding bed could be planted with plants that would partially hide the base of the stone. A suggested colour scheme is white and blue flowers, no more than 2½ feet (75cm) high with grey-leaved shrubs. The L-shaped border behind the sundial provides space for numerous plants, depending on the size,

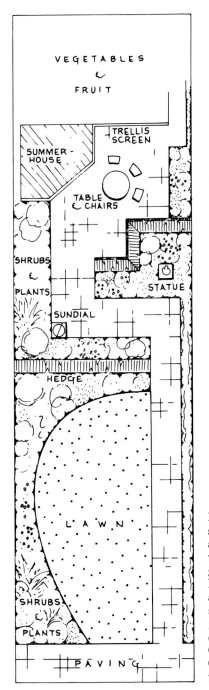

8 feet
2.5 metres

VEGETABLES
&
FRUIT

TRELLIS
SCREEN

SUMMER-
HOUSE

TABLE
& CHAIRS

SHRUBS
&
PLANTS

STATUE

SUNDIAL

HEDGE

LAWN

SHRUBS
&
PLANTS

PAVING

Plan 4: Two gardens in one narrow strip. By dividing the garden with a hedge a secluded area is created, with the result that the entire garden cannot be seen from the house. This method of dividing the area into 'rooms' has been successfully employed in many gardens, large and small; for first-class examples see Sissinghurst Castle, Kent, or Hidcote Manor, Gloucestershire, both owned by the National Trust.

Rhododendron williamsianum, a delightful dwarf species

conditions and aspect. In a cool lime-free soil a small collection of dwarf azaleas and rhododendrons interplanted with groups of lilies would be appropriate. Lilies are seen to advantage between low evergreens, the leaves of which seem to put the large blossoms into better proportion than the meagre foliage provided by the lilies themselves.

If rhododendrons will not grow some of the hardy fuchsias probably will, and the cultivars with large flowers which bloom from July onwards are 'Mrs Popple', 'Chillerton Beauty', 'Uncle Charlie' and 'Dr. Foster'. Earlier in the season colour can be introduced by interplanting with violets (see p.49) and dwarf bulbs.

At least some of the shrubs and plants near the sitting-out space in front of the summerhouse should be fragrant and the following cannot be overlooked; *Viburnum* × *juddii*, *Daphne* × *burkwoodii*, *Lonicera americana*, *Jasminum officinale* 'Affine'. A few plants bedded out annually, for the benefit of their scent and worth the trouble are tobacco plants, heliotrope and ten-week stocks.

Above: Lilies, such as *Lilium lancifolium*, go well with rhododendrons
Below: Jasmine should be planted where the scent can be appreciated

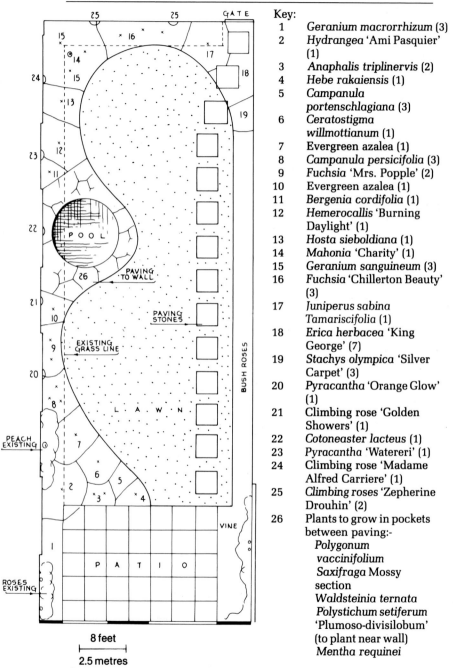

Key:
1   Geranium macrorrhizum (3)
2   Hydrangea 'Ami Pasquier' (1)
3   Anaphalis triplinervis (2)
4   Hebe rakaiensis (1)
5   Campanula portenschlagiana (3)
6   Ceratostigma willmottianum (1)
7   Evergreen azalea (1)
8   Campanula persicifolia (3)
9   Fuchsia 'Mrs. Popple' (2)
10 Evergreen azalea (1)
11 Bergenia cordifolia (1)
12 Hemerocallis 'Burning Daylight' (1)
13 Hosta sieboldiana (1)
14 Mahonia 'Charity' (1)
15 Geranium sanguineum (3)
16 Fuchsia 'Chillerton Beauty' (3)
17 Juniperus sabina Tamariscifolia (1)
18 Erica herbacea 'King George' (7)
19 Stachys olympica 'Silver Carpet' (3)
20 Pyracantha 'Orange Glow' (1)
21 Climbing rose 'Golden Showers' (1)
22 Cotoneaster lacteus (1)
23 Pyracantha 'Watereri' (1)
24 Climbing rose 'Madame Alfred Carriere' (1)
25 Climbing roses 'Zepherine Drouhin' (2)
26 Plants to grow in pockets between paving:-
    Polygonum vaccinifolium
    Saxifraga Mossy section
    Waldsteinia ternata
    Polystichum setiferum 'Plumoso-divisilobum' (to plant near wall)
    Mentha requinei

8 feet

2.5 metres

Plan 5: A bold outline is one way of dealing with a long, narrow garden. Here, sweeping curves create interest, and a pool acts as a focal point

40

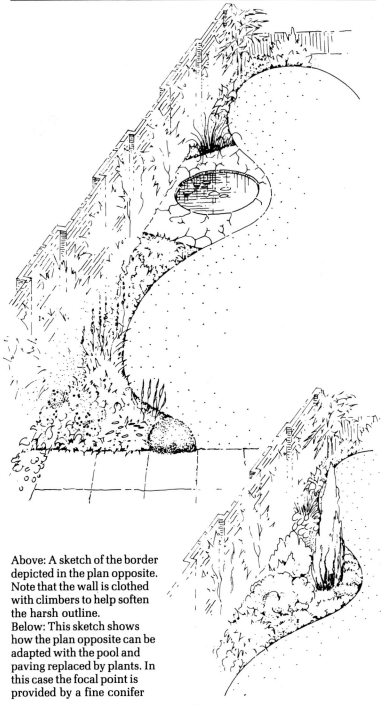

Above: A sketch of the border depicted in the plan opposite. Note that the wall is clothed with climbers to help soften the harsh outline.
Below: This sketch shows how the plan opposite can be adapted with the pool and paving replaced by plants. In this case the focal point is provided by a fine conifer

Bergenia 'Silberlicht', one of many fine examples of these excellent plants

---

Another narrow garden measuring 100 ft x 36 ft (30m x 11m) is depicted in plan 5 (see p.40), and in this instance there is the possibility that the high wall on the left would appear out of scale to the width of the garden.

The flower border was originally straight and it has now been brought out into a deep curve from the wall and by contrast recedes back again towards the wall making the bed in places very narrow. The idea behind this is that the variation in shape helps to balance the relative height of the boundary.

One of the primary objects of the design was to include a pool which is formal to the extent that it is circular although it is in an informal context flanked with crazy paving and low-growing plants between some of the crevices. The border is a mixture of shrubs and perennial plants. Not everyone wishes to have a pool in the garden and one very good reason often expressed is because of the danger to young children.

The sketch on page 41 illustrates the same border with a narrow conifer at the widest part of it; a good variety for this purpose is *Chamaecyparis lawsoniana* 'Ellwoodii', which forms a compact blue-grey column. It is fairly slow-growing eventually attaining about 16 ft (4.6m) but it has advantages over some other, larger, conifers that might outgrow the position. An elevation at this spot

Mahonia 'Charity' has fragrant yellow flowers

makes a focal point and has an influence on the garden design. It contrasts beautifully, for instance, with a carpet of winter- and summer-flowering heathers, or plants to give similar effect such as *Polygonum vacciniifolium* which will grow in a soil unsuitable for heathers.

A shrub that can also be used as an accent plant is *Mahonia* 'Charity' with a sturdy upright habit which reaches 8 ft (2.5 m) in height; the leaflets of the elegant foot long ash-like foliage give a striking architectural effect and in blossom it is one of the joys of early winter.

Plan 6 (see p.46) illustrates a design for a garden only 20 ft (6m) in width but with the use of curved and oblique lines the parallel boundaries are largely hidden. It will be seen that there too the paving near the house does not have to be straight-sided and the outline integrates with the garden.

The area near the plum tree is partly hidden and gives a feeling of seclusion, the arrangement of the lattice screen at right angles from the left boundary presents a direct view of the bed running obliquely across the garden.

Space for fruit is well represented and certain selected salad crops and vegetables could be grown.

43

Above: The model 'town garden' at Wisley
Opposite, above: Arbours and statues create focal points
Opposite, below: Day lilies are good herbaceous plants – this is
Hemerocallis 'Linda'

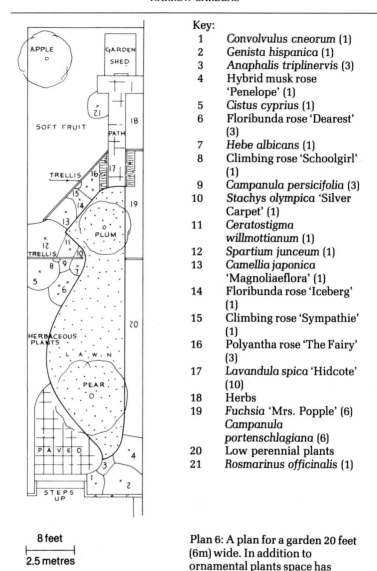

Key:
1   *Convolvulus cneorum* (1)
2   *Genista hispanica* (1)
3   *Anaphalis triplinervis* (3)
4   Hybrid musk rose 'Penelope' (1)
5   *Cistus cyprius* (1)
6   Floribunda rose 'Dearest' (3)
7   *Hebe albicans* (1)
8   Climbing rose 'Schoolgirl' (1)
9   *Campanula persicifolia* (3)
10 *Stachys olympica* 'Silver Carpet' (1)
11 *Ceratostigma willmottianum* (1)
12 *Spartium junceum* (1)
13 *Camellia japonica* 'Magnoliaeflora' (1)
14 Floribunda rose 'Iceberg' (1)
15 Climbing rose 'Sympathie' (1)
16 Polyantha rose 'The Fairy' (3)
17 *Lavandula spica* 'Hidcote' (10)
18 Herbs
19 *Fuchsia* 'Mrs. Popple' (6) *Campanula portenschlagiana* (6)
20 Low perennial plants
21 *Rosmarinus officinalis* (1)

8 feet
2.5 metres

Plan 6: A plan for a garden 20 feet (6m) wide. In addition to ornamental plants space has been left for fruit and herbs

Opposite above: *Polygonum affine* 'Dimity', a useful carpeting plant
Opposite below: Room can always be found for a striking foliage plant like *Hosta fortunei* 'Albopicta'

Agapanthus produce striking blue flowers in summer (see p.36)

Above: *Lavandula stoechas*, French lavender, likes full sun
Below: *Viola odorata*, sweet violet, a useful plant for ground cover

Fruit and Vegetables

In a very small garden it is doubtful if space-consuming vegetables, such as potatoes, are worth growing, and items that give a good return and occupy less room are to be preferred. Lettuce are easily grown and there is no comparison between one that is freshly cut and another that has had its growth terminated some time previously. It is also exciting to grow some of the less common items that are not usually seen in the shops, such as globe artichokes and sugar peas, and if you have a small greenhouse aubergines, tomatoes and sweet peppers may also be raised.

Runner beans have the great advantage of thriving on the same site from one year to the next provided the ground is fed. When runner beans are supported by a pyramid of canes or similar means, the blossom and bold foliage of the vines can produce an attractive elevation in the flower garden. The foliage of beetroot is sometimes a useful foil for flowers, while another plant with spectacular colours and delicious to eat is spinach beet which can be grown in flower borders or in the vegetable garden.

Apples and pears can be conveniently grown as cordons (a cordon is a form of tree trained to a single stem) when space is at a premium (see p.52), and a good position is often adjacent to a path where they receive light and air, and pruning and spraying can be done easily at the appropriate times. A judicious selection of cultivars should be able to provide the family with both cooking and eating apples throughout the winter and spring. Trained plum trees are usually grown against a framework of wires and canes or against a wall or fence. If soft fruit is grown, necessitating a cage, it might be preferable to put all the fruit under protective netting. An example of the fruit section of a small garden may be seen in the family garden at the Society's garden in Wisley (see p.21). A diagram of the fruit and vegetable section of this garden is given opposite. For detailed advice on growing and harvesting fruit and vegetables see *The Fruit Garden Displayed* and *The Vegetable Garden Displayed*, both of which are published by The Royal Horticultural Society.

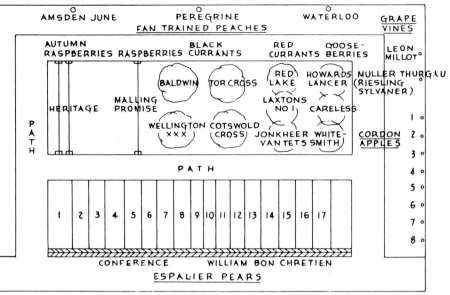

The fruit and vegetable section of the 'family garden' (see pp. 21 & 27)

Key (to diagram above)

Cordon Apples.
1. Sturmer Pippin
2. Ashmead's Kernel
3. Golden Delicious
4. Cox's Orange Pippin
5. Egremont Russet
6. Lord Lambourne
7. James Grieve
8. Red George Cave

Vegetables.
1. (Seed Bed)
2. Tomato 'Pixie'
3. Onion sets 'Stuttgarter Giant'
4. French bean 'Sprite'
5. Spinach beet 'Perpetual'
6. Salad onion 'White Lisbon'
7. Lettuce 'Unrivalled'
8. Beetroot 'Little Ball'
9. Lettuce 'Fortune'
10. Brussels sprouts 'Peer Gynt'
11. Cabbage 'Hidena'
12. Carrot Nantes - Champion 'Scarlet Horn'
13. Parsnip 'Hollow Crown'
14. Courgette 'Green Bush F'
15. Cabbage 'Hispi'
16. Broad Bean 'Kordrin'
17. Potato 'Foremost'

Opposite: Cordon apples take up little space and produce a good crop of fruit; pears can also be grown in this way
Above: Plants will grow in small pockets among paving stones

Paved Gardens

The gardens in many city situations are often very small and secluded by walls on all sides. It is usually preferable to keep the design formal although not necessarily employing a repetition of pattern, but one of balance. Plan 7 (opposite) represents a very small garden 28 ft x 28 ft (9m x 9m) and the beds are retained on three different levels, the small figure in the left corner being at the highest point.

Having laid down the basis of the design in the shape of the walls, which are of quite low elevation, one is left with a fairly flexible choice of plants and shrubs even if, as is sometimes the case, the garden is shaded by buildings. In locations such as these

Good use made of walls in a small garden

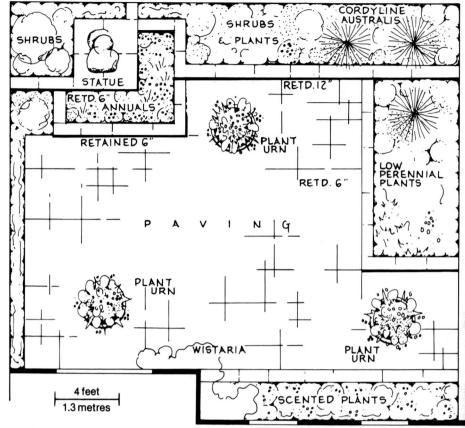

Plan 7: In a tiny area greater interest is introduced by beds on different levels. This garden measures 28 × 24 ft (8.5 × 7m); focal points are created both architecturally and with plants

the temperature is often several degrees higher than in the open countryside and some less hardy and unusual plants thrive happily. Interest through the year can be maintained with foliage of different colour and texture, low perennials, annuals and bulbs.

The introduction of a formal pool is shown in plan 8 (see pp. 58 & 59) in a different context and the intention is to fit it into the concept of a semi-naturalized garden and relate it to the existing paving.

In this case, it was useless to try and match the weathered stone that had been down for some years and therefore broken paving was used to unify adverse composition of material and pattern. Both plans produce the same objective but one is for a smaller layout and the same features are represented in each.

Above: *Convolvulus cneorum*, rue, and ivy mingle well together
Opposite: Pink, blue and silver creates an effective colour scheme

Below and opposite above: Plan 8, two versions. Designs for relating a
formal pool to an existing patio in a naturalized garden (see p.55).
In this case broken paving was used to match the stone that was already
in situ, but it should be remembered that a very wide range of paving
materials exists today. Examples to choose from include bricks (of many
different types and colours), concrete, stone, reconstituted stone and
gravel of different grades

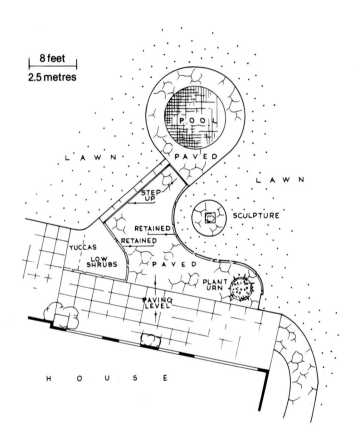

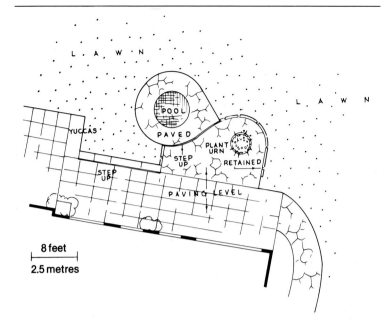

8 feet

2.5 metres

Below: Sketch of the pool featured in the plan opposite

The usual characteristic of most corner sites is to see a boundary line running obliquely across the view and in this case, as in other gardens, we should try to take advantage of the longest aspect which in these situations is towards the point where the boundaries meet.

In plan 9 (below) I have produced a lawn that takes almost

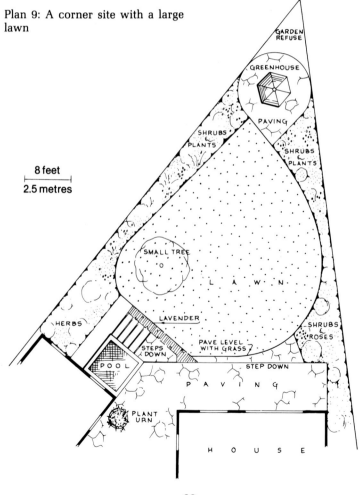

Plan 9: A corner site with a large lawn

GARDEN REFUSE

GREENHOUSE

PAVING

SHRUBS & PLANTS

SHRUBS & PLANTS

8 feet
2.5 metres

SMALL TREE

L A W N

HERBS

LAVENDER

SHRUBS & ROSES

STEPS DOWN

PAVE LEVEL WITH GRASS

POOL

STEP DOWN

P A V I N G

PLANT URN

H O U S E

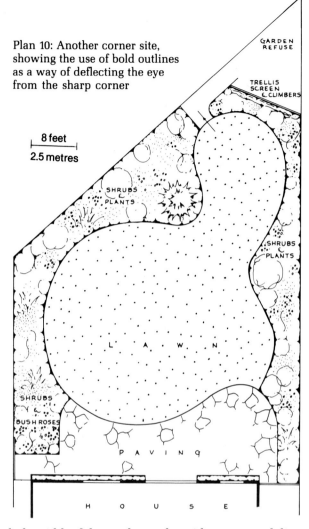

Plan 10: Another corner site, showing the use of bold outlines as a way of deflecting the eye from the sharp corner

8 feet
2.5 metres

GARDEN REFUSE

TRELLIS SCREEN & CLIMBERS

SHRUBS & PLANTS

SHRUBS & PLANTS

SHRUBS & BUSH ROSES

L A W N

P A V I N G

H O U S E

the whole width of the garden at the widest part, and diverted the eye towards the architectural structure of a hexagonal greenhouse and away from the boundary that runs obliquely across the view. The small tree on the left side also deflects the eye towards the right.

Plan 10 (above) also illustrates a similar situation but designed with a somewhat different approach. The line of the paving near the house is part of a continuous outline of the lawn which extends in a deep curve to a prominent convex curve towards the centre of the garden. The apex of the bed is given emphasis by an upright shrub or small tree or an architectural feature and the storage space and garden refuse is screened with panels of square lattice up which climbing plants can be grown.

Three Different Gardens

The gardens represented in plans 11, 12 and 13 incorporate features that are common to the needs of many gardens. The first plan (below) is that of a garden above the patio and the higher ground is retained by a low wall 2 ft (60cm) in height with access

Plan 11: Paved areas and a lawn

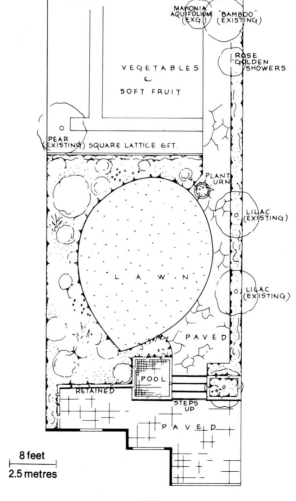

MAHONIA AQUIFOLIUM (EXG)

"BAMBOO" (EXISTING)

VEGETABLES & SOFT FRUIT

ROSE GOLDEN SHOWERS

PEAR (EXISTING) SQUARE LATTICE 6FT.

PLANT URN

LILAC (EXISTING)

LAWN

LILAC (EXISTING)

PAVED

POOL

RETAINED

STEPS UP

PAVED

8 feet

2.5 metres

to it by four steps. If water is to be part of the design I think this situation is ideal for a formal raised pool, retained by the wall at the front, level with the soil and with paving at the back and sides. This allows plants to grow over the edges and the pool is close enough to the house for the pond life to be enjoyed even from indoors. The paved area above the steps gives a feeling of spaciousness combined with the lawn and adds further room for tables and chairs.

The garden depicted in plan 12 (see p.64) is relatively narrow compared with the length, 25 feet (7.6m). Specific focal points have been created to distract the eye from a view straight down the garden; a curved path and divided lawn help to disguise the long, narrow nature of the plot.

In a shaded patio at the side of the house, plant containers hold foliage plants that include *Fatsia japonica, Euonymus fortunei radicans* 'Silver Queen', dwarf *Arundinaria* and *Phormium,* whilst blossom is contributed by *Impatiens* and *Begonia semperflorens.* Also near the house a pool is balanced by a plant urn on the opposite side with an accent of colour provided by spring and summer flowers. A fountain is well placed either as a single jet or bell fountain in the centre of the pool. About half way down the garden on the left side a birdbath emphasises the apex of the border and the lawn at this point narrows to 8 feet (2.5m) wide before terminating at a screen of climbing plants to hide the vegetable section and buildings beyond.

When the garden is a foot or two above the ground floor of the house, as it is in plan 13 (see p.65), the basic layout and plant material needs careful consideration. In this garden the existing retaining wall was a short distance from the windows and constructed straight across from one side to the other and gave a feeling that it was inadequate to prevent the garden encroaching towards the house.

To modify this impression the design is aligned in one direction and the patio shape is altered by changing the line of the wall; the actual area of paving remains about the same by taking a corner off the lower right side and extending it on the left to produce a longer view of the patio in this direction. The choice of shrubs and plants is important in a garden that is on a higher level or a garden that slopes upwards away from the house. It becomes apparent that, for example, upright bush roses or some of the taller perennials when planted too near a house, not only obscure the garden but also ensure that the most visible part of the plants is the lower part of the stems with the result that the effect of the flowers is lost. Taller planting on the sides, leaving the centre open, would form a framework for the rest of the garden.

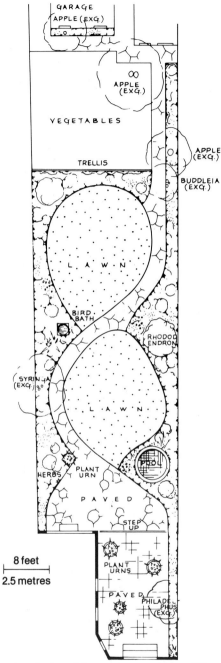

GARAGE
APPLE (EXG.)

APPLE
(EXG.)

VEGETABLES

APPLE
(EXG.)

TRELLIS

BUDDLEIA
(EXG.)

L A W N

BIRD
BATH

RHODOD
ENDRON

SYRIN-A
(EXG.) 80°

L A W N

HERBS

PLANT
URN

POOL

P A V E D

STEP
UP

8 feet

PLANT
URNS

2.5 metres

P A V E D

PHILADE-
PHUS
(EXG.)

Plan 12: A garden designed for easy access (see p. 63)

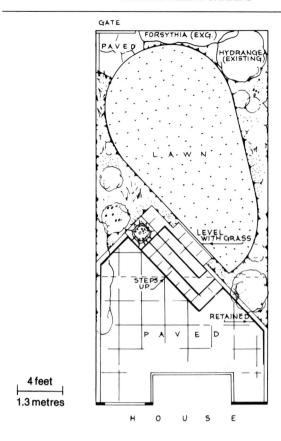

GATE

FORSYTHIA (EXG.)

PAVED

HYDRANGEA (EXISTING)

L A W N

LEVEL WITH GRASS

STEPS UP

RETAINED

P A V E D

4 feet

1.3 metres

H O U S E

Above: Plan 13 makes use of oblique angles to give an appearance of space (see p. 63)
Below: A sketch showing the effect created by the plan above

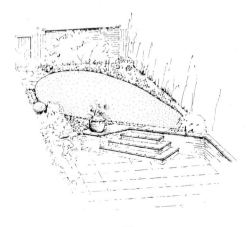

A North-Facing Garden

Except on particularly hot days in summer, sitting on a permanently shady side of the house (in this country) is usually too cool for comfort, and those seeking relaxation are likely to want to sit in a sunnier and warmer part of the garden. Plan 14 (opposite) is of a north-facing site with the ground sloping up from the house. The doors and windows look out on to a comparatively small paved area from which a way leads off to other parts of the garden.

The top right hand corner is a sun-trap and a level plateau has been made to form a circular paved area there, ringed with a wide grass verge, the total width being 20 feet (6m). On the side nearest the house the ground is retained by a wall, the top of which is level, or just below, the grass behind it and terminates in the natural slope at both ends. The plateau is perfectly flat and a comfortable place to arrange table and chairs with a view of the garden sloping away in three directions. A terrace is sometimes difficult to design, even if a level part of the garden is available, and to make it aesthetically acceptable and also functional a curved wall built in this way sometimes provides the solution.

The way up from the patio is by a gradual slope, partly grassed, with paving stones laid level with the lawn along the edge of the border. This provides a dry path to the terrace and plants near the front of the bed can sprawl at random without being damaged by the grass mower.

The design at the front of the house is one of extreme simplicity and it is based on a single curved line which embodies a paved section between the drive and front door. The approach to the house should I think have a look of welcome. All too often the emphasis is on the garage and the entrance to the front door is provided by a very secondary little path.

In this design the small front lawn is edged with low-growing shrubs which can be enjoyed by anyone waiting at the front door. Suitable shrubs for this sunnier part of the garden might include lavender (see p. 49) and *Lavatera olbia*.

Opposite: Plan 14 provides a place in the sun in a north-facing garden

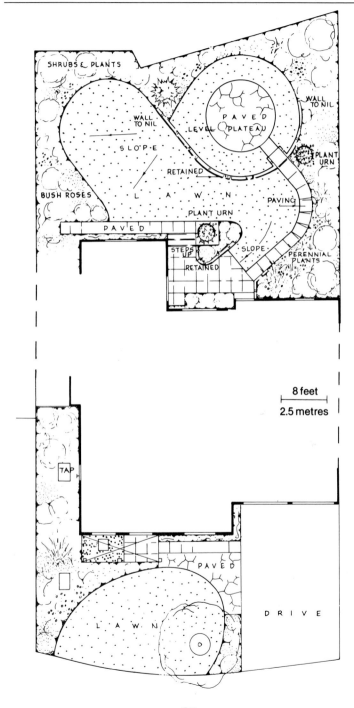

SHRUBS & PLANTS

WALL TO NIL

WALL TO NIL

PAVED LEVEL PLATEAU

WALL TO NIL

SLOPE

PLANT URN

RETAINED

BUSH ROSES

L A W N

PAVING

PLANT URN

PAVED

PAVING

STEPS UP

SLOPE

RETAINED

PERENNIAL PLANTS

8 feet

2.5 metres

TAP

PAVED

L A W N

D R I V E

The design in plan 15 (opposite) is for a garden larger than the two preceding plots although it is a size typical of many gardens of today.

The outer sides of the garden are already constructed and the new cultivated sections consist of one fairly large island bed and another that is smaller. The design is again based on oblique lines and the feature of the garden is that it is possible to walk in different directions without seeing other parts at the same time.

The planting in the smaller island bed forms a substantial grouping of shrubs and balances similar elevations in the opposite border. This layout frames a view of a plant urn backed by a yew hedge in one direction and looking in the other there is a carefully chosen sculpture placed amongst bush roses, although it could equally well have been amongst the soft colours of herbaceous plants. Another view of the urn is between the existing border on the right side and the other straight side of the island bed, adding another dimension to the garden. It is the different aspects and association of line within a pattern of continuity that contributes to the overall design.

Erica herbacea 'Vivellii' forms dense hummocks

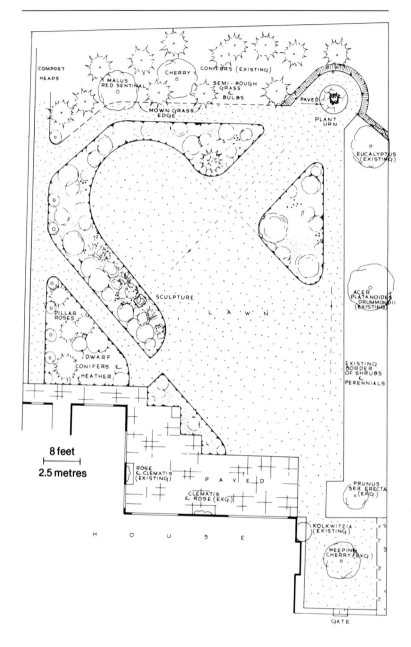

Plan 15. A garden incorporating several points of focal interest, for example an ornamental urn and a sculpture

A Rose Garden

For the owner of a small garden roses are frequently grouped in separate beds or borders and contribute an abundance of blossom throughout the summer. Technically all roses are shrubs and many have found a permanent place in plant lists for mixed borders.

All the floribundas (cluster-flowered) are extremely useful in a mixed border of evergreen and deciduous shrubs and some perennial plants. The rose 'Queen Elizabeth' for example will tower 6 feet (1.8 m) or more at the back of the border; its counterpart 'Scarlet Queen Elizabeth', 'Iceberg' (white) and 'Chinatown' (yellow) are also roses for the back of the border. Nearer the front of the bed some shorter cultivars such as 'Elizabeth of Glamis', 'Intrigue' and 'Allgold' produce a succession of pink, crimson and yellow flowers, in bloom from June to October.

Hybrid tea roses (large-flowered) differ in that they rarely look comfortable in the mixed population of a shrub border, except perhaps certain very strong growers such as 'Buccaneer', 'Peace', 'Eden Rose' and 'Uncle Walter', and in fact it can be said that these plants, because of their size, are difficult to place in beds of shorter roses. In some rose gardens it is the practice to plant each bed with one colour and on a sufficiently large scale the effect is magnificent. When bush roses are part of the general layout, however, sometimes one of the most appropriate places for hybrid teas is within the lines of walls and paths where they help to create a semi-formal concept and do not look out of place.

Rose cultivars in the foreground near the house should not be tall growers because not only will the bushes obscure the view but the heights are out of scale for beds say 4 to 5 feet wide (1.2 to 1.5m). Different colours are often grown in the same bed and the most satisfactory result is usually obtained by planting groups of one colour and taking care to choose cultivars that are about equal in vigour.

Plan 16 (opposite) is for a rose garden of rather unconventional design occupying an area of about 80 by 30 feet (25 by 9m) – the size of many small gardens, although the plan shown is part of a larger garden with a secluded section for roses. A feature about the layout is that although it is effective as a rose garden it could also be taken as a design for a small ornamental garden and

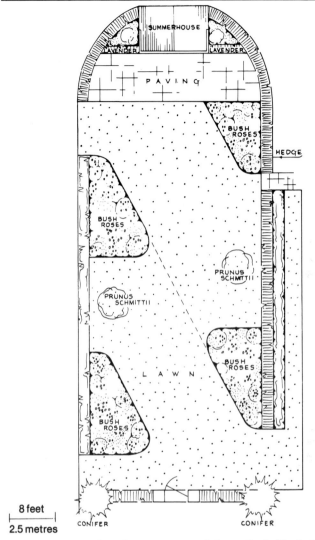

Plan 16: A rose garden of unconventional shape. Probably the best way to get ideas for rose borders is to visit the gardens of the Royal National Rose Society near St Albans

instead of planting only roses, shrubs and perennials could also be grown. Whichever planting scheme is adopted the shape of the beds produces an enlarging effect on the garden and the actual clear space through the centre is 11 feet (3.3m) which will appear to elongate the distance to the summer-house from the gate. A similar effect looking from the other end, and the shaping of the beds, partially obscures sections of the grass in which two upright growing flowering cherry trees are planted. If all four are not devoted to roses two opposite sections could be planted with shrubs and perennials. Planted as a rose garden the beds are large enough to take enough bushes to give a good display of colour and one might be content to restrict the choice to four cultivars, or possibly as previously mentioned, several groups of different colours in each bed. The areas of blossom seen from eye-level will appear closer together than on the plan, because the view of the beds is foreshortened, so there is far less visible break between one bed and another producing a greater mass of colour from the paving in front of the summer-house and other parts of the garden.

'*Parkdirektor Riggers*', a climbing rose trained as a pillar

A Front Garden

The layout of the garden in front of a house is not always taken to its full potential and yet it is supposed to be the first welcoming introduction to the home. The approach to the house, from the moment of crossing the boundary, should leave no doubt about the direction of the front door. The commonest and most regrettable mistake is to have an impressive expanse of concrete or asphalt leading towards the garage and a small insignificant path at right angles going to the house. The path should be as wide and spacious as possible within the proportions of the garden, creating a feeling of being drawn towards the front entrance.

The garden in plan 17 was designed with these requirements in mind. The paving slabs are set in a scree of shingle, into which rock plants and a few heathers may be planted with charming effect. The entrance to the garage cannot be overlooked, even if it

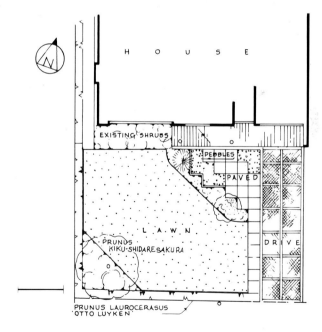

Plan 17: A front garden, using several materials to produce different textures

A mixture of paving and shingle dotted with low-growing plants

is not the most aesthetic feature of the garden. However, a large area of hard material can be improved by using bricks to make square divisions infilled with paving, concrete setts or textured concrete (see also p. 24). Another example of this technique is given in plan 21 (p. 84), which shows the forecourt of a listed building. It has been designed to include a parking space, using bricks similar in colour to the house to make the intrusion of modern necessities more acceptable. Paving is inlaid between the brick divisions, which measure 4 by 4 feet (1.2 × 1.2 m).

A Garden in Shade

A large number of our garden plants have been introduced from other parts of the world and most are remarkably tolerant of the vagaries of the British climate. Some are particularly useful, delighting in more open parts of the garden but being not averse to shaded positions.

There are various degrees of shade. While many plants, such as border phlox, erigeron, hosta, aquilegia and certain roses, are happy on the north side of a wall, the choice is much more selective under a close covering of trees, where the soil is often dry and impoverished by the roots. Even the density of the tree canopy varies and plants which might grow perfectly well beneath the light open branches of a false acacia will not survive under the thick foliage of a sycamore. The nature of the soil, whether acid or alkaline, dry or moist, is also critical.

Plan 18 (p. 77) represents an imaginary garden in three possible combinations of shade and soil type, with three tables of appropriate plants corresponding to these different situations. Table 1 gives plants that should succeed in total shade in slightly alkaline or neutral soil. More usually, however, one or other side of the garden receives a limited amount of sun and table 2 therefore lists plants suitable for partial shade. In these more favourable conditions, a number of colourful shrubs can be recommended to replace some of the more sombre evergreens and groups of naturalized bulbs, such as aconites, snowdrops and chionodoxa, could be established between the larger plants.

Table 3 is a planting scheme for moist acid soil in semi-shade and includes rhododendrons, azaleas and hydrangeas. Hortensia and lacecap hydrangeas resent dryness at the roots and will revel in such a situation, producing their flowerheads in shades of blue and purple. Table 4 contains suggested plants for dense shade under trees.

Overleaf above: The colourful long-spurred *Aquilegia* hybrids flower in early summer and seed themselves freely (see table 2, p. 78)

Overleaf below: *Camellia japonica* 'Magnoliiflora', a beautiful medium-sized shrub of compact habit, will thrive in semi-shade on acid or neutral soil (see table 3, p. 78)

Plan 18: A garden in shade, illustrating three different conditions of shade

Table 1: Total shade

Number on plan

1	Bergenia 'Ballawley'
2	1 Rubus calycinoides
3	1 Polystichum setiferum 'Divisilobum'
4	1 Vinca minor 'Bowles' Variety'
5	3 Epimedium × warleyense
6	2 Hosta fortunei
7	1 Euonymus fortunei 'Silver Queen'
8	1 Viburnum tinus 'Variegatum'
9	1 Mahonia aquifolium
10	5 Impatiens F$_1$ hybrids for summer, dwarf tulips for spring
11	3 Epimedium grandiflorum 'Rose Queen'
12	1 Sarcococca confusa and 5 Lamium maculatum 'Beacon Silver'
13	3 Anemone × hybrida 'September Charm'
14	3 Tiarella wherryi
15	7 Impatiens F$_1$ hybrids for summer, dwarf tulips fo spring
16	1 Elaeagnus × ebbingei 'Gilt Edge'
17	3 Viburnum davidii
18	1 Brunnera microphylla
19	1 Iris foetidissima
20	1 Aucuba japonica 'Crotonifolia'
21	3 Cyclamen purpurascens (C.europaeum)
22	1 Laurus nobilis
23	1 Cephalotaxus harringtonia 'Fastigiata'
24	9 Impatiens F$_1$ hybrids for summer, dwarf tulips for spring
25	2 Mahonia aquifolium
26	Skimmia japonica 'Foremanii'
27	3 Astrantia major
28	1 Daphne lanceolata
29	1 Helleborus lividus corsicus
30	1 Geranium macrorrhizum
31	3 Brunnera microphylla
32	1 Danae racemosa
33	3 Anemone × hybrida 'Bressingham Glow'
34	3 Tellima grandiflora 'Purpurea'
35	9 Impatiens F$_1$ hybrids
36	3 Viola odorata
	3 Asarum caudatum
	3 Cyclamen hederifolium
	3 Cyclamen hederifolium 'Album'
	3 Pulmonaria rubra 'Bowles' Variety'
37	1 Fatsia japonica
38	1 Hedera colchica 'Dentata Variegata'

39	1 climbing rose 'Madam Alfred Carrière'		33	1 *Fuchsia* 'Mrs Popple'
40	1 *Jasminum nudiflorum*		34	
41	1 climbing rose 'Mermaid'		35	9 *Begonia semperflorens*
42	1 *Hedera helix* 'Glacier'		36	
43	1 *Jasminum nudiflorum*		37	
44	1 climbing rose 'Zephirine Drouhin'		38	1 *Pyracantha* 'Watereri'
45	1 *Choisya ternata*		39	1 climbing rose 'Golden Showers'
			40	1 *Pyracantha* 'Golden Dome'
			41	
			42	
			43	1 *Cotoneaster lacteus*

Table 2: Partial shade

Number on plan

1	(see table 1 where no name is given)
2	
3	
4	
5	
6	3 *Fuchsia* 'Alice Hoffmann'
7	
8	
9	1 *Daphne retusa*
10	
11	
12	1 *Mahonia japonica*
13	
14	
15	
16	
17	3 hybrid musk roses 'Penelope'
18	
19	
20	1 *Ilex × altaclerense* 'Golden King'
21	
22	
23	
24	5 bush floribunda (cluster-flowered) roses 'Dearest'
25	1 *Weigela florida* 'Variegata'
26	
27	3 *Astilbe × arendsii* 'Fire'
28	3 hybrid musk roses 'Felicia'
29	
30	
31	5 *Aquilegia* long-spurred hybrids
32	1 *Chaenomeles speciosa* 'Simonii'

Table 3: Partial shade and acid soil

Number on plan

1	1 *Andromeda polifolia* 'Compacta'
2	1 *Gaultheria procumbens*
3	(see table 1 where no name is given)
4	
5	
6	3 *Fuchsia* 'Alice Hoffmann'
7	
8	1 *Rhododendron* 'Doncaster'
9	1 *Daphne retusa*
10	
11	
12	3 *Rhododendron* Exbury hybrids
13	
14	
15	
16	1 *Rhododendron* 'Mrs G. W. Leak'
17	3 *Hydrangea* 'Blue Wave'
18	
19	
20	
21	
22	1 *Hamamelis mollis*
23	1 *Laurus nobilis*
24	
25	2 *Rhododendron* 'Blaauw's Pink'
26	3 *Hydrangea* 'Lanarth White'
27	
28	1 *Camellia japonica* 'Magnoliiflora'
29	

A subtle blend of colours in the shade garden at Bressingham Hall, Norfolk

30
31 5 *Aquilegia* long-spurred
      hybrids
32 3 *Rhododendron*
      'Irohayama'
33 1 *Fuchsia* 'Mrs Popple'
34
35
36
37
38
39
40
41
42
43

Table 4: Dense shade under trees

Arundinaria japonica
Arundinaria murielae
Aucuba japonica and cultivars
Buxus sempervirens
Fatsia japonica
Mahonia aquifolium
Rubus odoratus
Ruscus hypoglossum
Sarcococca confusa
Symphoricarpos × *chenaultii* 'Hancock'
Symphoricarpos × *doorenbosii* cultivars

A Garden on a Slope

A garden on a hill, with land either rising upward from the house or dropping away from it, has different problems to one on a level site. If the slope is gentle, the garden can probably be designed without altering the natural fall of the land, or a simple form of terracing could be undertaken which does not require excessive removal of earth, to produce a flat area of grass or paving.

However, for a garden on a steeper slope some consideration should be given to the heights and shapes of plants. As a general rule, where the ground rises from the viewpoint, it is preferable to have mostly fairly low plants, while on a downward incline, it is better to have tall plants in strategic places to avoid the feeling that the garden is slipping away. This can be seen most effectively on the hillsides in Italy, with narrow pencil-like cypresses appearing to almost peg the landscape in position.

Plan 19 illustrates a garden with a steep rise from the house to a more level section at the top, which is given over to a children's play area and space for growing vegetables and fruit. The original centre path has been replaced by a zig-zag path ascending from the lawn near the house and this forms a series of informal sloping terraces retained by low walls. The planting scheme in the centre part of the garden is based on low-growing plants and spreading shrubs, while larger plants are allowed at the sides and near the top to screen the vegetables and fruit. The paths are made of non-slip cream-coloured concrete setts and the patios in front of the house and summerhouse are of reconstituted rectangular paving.

The garden shown on plan 20 (p. 83) falls steeply to the lower boundary. It is rarely satisfactory for the garden to slope immediately away from the house and a flat level area should be made, even if it is relatively small, to provide a firm safe place for sitting and viewing the garden. The curved retaining wall gives a structural outline to the design and grass descends on each side to the lower lawn. Several small mature fruit trees have been kept to create much needed height and along the lower boundary a number of medium-sized conifers and eucalyptus will form an evergreen screen of varied texture and colour. Eucalyptus responds well to pruning every two years to restrict height and encourage thick bushy growth.

The shape of the lawn results in beds of different widths,

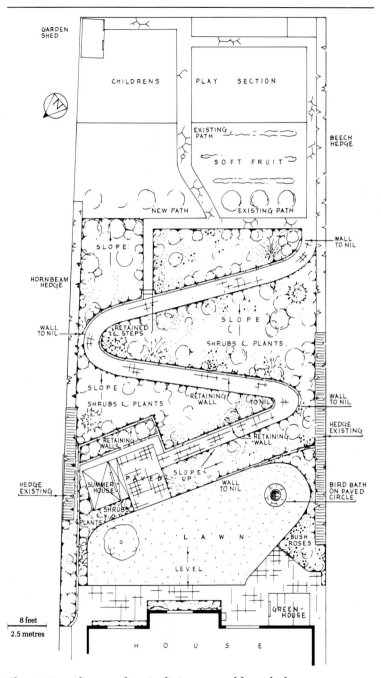

GARDEN
SHED

CHILDRENS   PLAY   SECTION

EXISTING
PATH

BEECH
HEDGE

SOFT FRUIT

NEW PATH   EXISTING PATH

WALL
TO NIL

SLOPE

HORNBEAM
HEDGE

WALL
TO NIL

SLOPE

RETAINED
& STEPS

SHRUBS & PLANTS

SLOPE

SHRUBS & PLANTS

RETAINING
WALL

TO NIL

WALL
TO NIL

HEDGE
EXISTING

RETAINING
WALLS

RETAINING
WALL

PAVED   SLOPE
UP

WALL
TO NIL

BIRD BATH
ON PAVED
CIRCLE

HEDGE
EXISTING

SUMMER
HOUSE

SHRUBS
& PLANTS

LAWN

BUSH
ROSES

LEVEL

GREEN-
HOUSE

8 feet

2.5 metres

H   O   U   S   E

Plan 19: A garden on a slope inclining upward from the house

An example of successful planting in a hillside garden

offering scope for imaginative planting with plants that require various situations, whether cool shade or full sun. The continuous line around the lawn detracts from the actual boundaries, while the sundial makes a focal point of interest and gives depth to the design.

Large banks in awkward situations present a special problem. Here, as I have recommended before, climbing plants are very valuable in providing a cover, enabling one to dispense with grass and the need to cut it. The plants are spaced about 4 feet (1.2 m) apart near the top of the bank and allowed to ramble without support, quickly forming a dense cascading mat. A shrub that immediately comes to mind is *Lonicera japonica* 'Halliana', a semi-evergreen honeysuckle with scented biscuit-coloured flowers, which will spread 15 to 20 feet (4.5–6 m). Similarly, *L. japonica* 'Aureoreticulata', a honeysuckle mainly grown for its

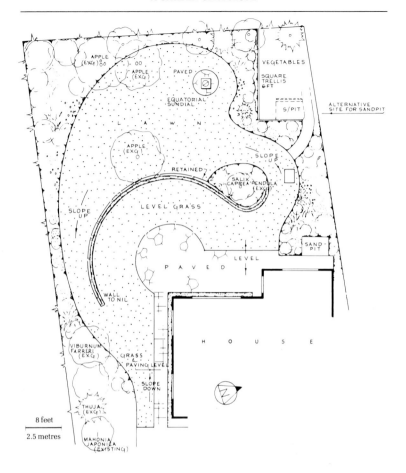

Plan 20: A garden on a slope falling away steeply from the house

variegated leaves, is excellent for the purpose. In places where other plants are reluctant to grow, *Hedera colchica* 'Dentata Variegata' might be the solution, either in shade under trees or in the open, and produces a carpet of large brightly variegated leaves over a wide area.

It may be almost impossible to actually plant in a very steep bank or cliff. However, many strong-growing climbers can be used in such a situation. They include *Polygonum baldschuanicum* (see p. 85), which should be planted away from trees; *Clematis montana* and its cultivars; *Parthenocissus quinquefolia*; and, in mild localities, *Meuhlenbeckia complexa*, which has delicate minute round leaves on thin wiry stems and will hang down like a curtain.

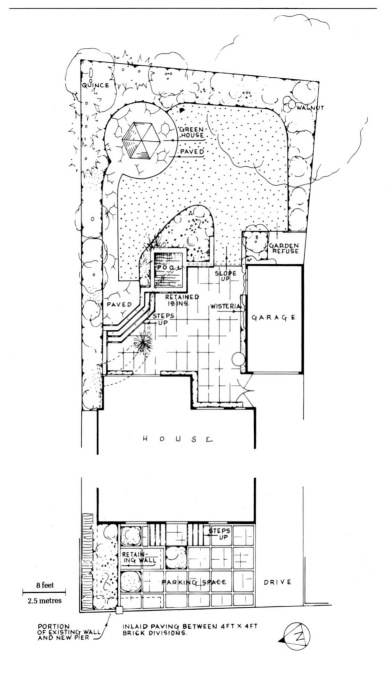

Plan 21: A garden on a slope rising from the house

Left: A curved retaining wall at the foot of a sloping bed

Right: The Russian vine, *Polygonum baldschuanicum*, is excellent for clothing a steep bank and flowers throughout summer and autumn

The garden in plan 21 is another site which slopes upwards from the house. The depth of gradient between the patio and the lawn is about 2 feet (60 cm), retained by a wall $1\frac{1}{2}$ feet (45 cm) high. The steps are seen at an angle from the house on the left side of the garden, interrelating with the walling and the raised pool, and the greenhouse is an added feature to complete the picture. (The forecourt at the front of the house is mentioned on p. 74.)

An Alternative to a Lawn

It is often said that even in the smallest garden there should be room for a lawn, however tiny, and I am not advocating a reversal of this principle, nor suggesting that a lawn should be abandoned without careful reflection. However, there are certain circumstances where it may be impractical to maintain a lawn and where the possible alternatives should be considered.

In plan 22 (overleaf) the grass has been replaced with shingle, while access to different parts of the garden is provided by the paving. A gradual upwards slope away from the house leads to a terrace at the north end with chairs and a table, where the owner may take advantage of a few sunny hours. The thickness of the shingle scree depends on the size of the pebbles. Aggregate of up to ¾ inch (20 mm) could be laid to a depth of about 2 inches (5 cm), giving a pleasant textured effect with the paving. Larger stones are more difficult to walk on and cannot be tucked round the stems of plants rooted in the soil underneath.

It is important to ensure first that all weeds are eradicated from the site and the ground should be made level and consolidated by rolling or treading in the same way as when preparing a lawn. The actual planting is not difficult. Having decided on the planting positions, a small area of pebbles is removed and laid aside and the soil excavated to a depth of 9 to 10 inches (25 cm) and 12 inches (30 cm) wide, replacing it with prepared compost suitable for the requirements of the plant. This should also be mixed into the sides of the hole and into the natural soil at the bottom. The plants are then inserted and the pebbles replaced closely around them. This scree effect is relatively simple to achieve, compared with a proper scree bed specially designed for those choice flora which flourish in broken rock and debris. There is a fine example of this type of moraine in the new alpine house at the RHS Garden, Wisley.

Planting in the scree brings a soft informal theme to the garden. Shrubs like *Juniperus communis* 'Repanda', *Rubus calycinoides*

Above: Scree beds at the Hillier Garden, Hampshire – an idea that can be easily adapted by the ordinary gardener

Below: A small pool fits nicely into an expanse of shingle and allows greater variety in planting (see p. 91)

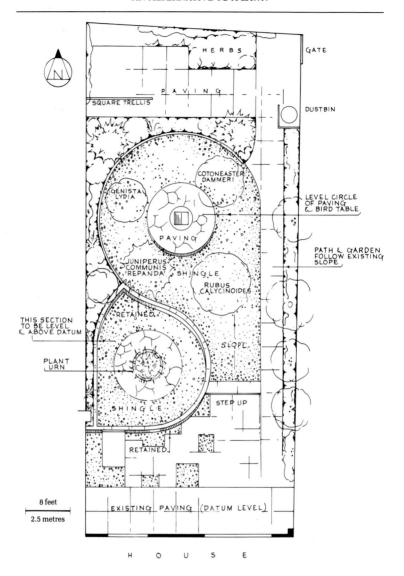

Plan 22: An alternative to a lawn, with shrubs growing in shingle scree

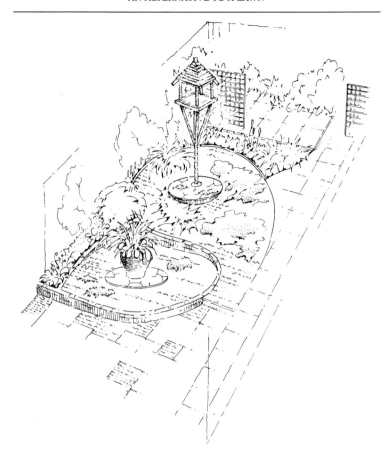

Sketch of the garden in plan 22

and *Cotoneaster dammeri* will grow through the pebbles and cover large sections with flat rug-like branches. Within a year or two the shingle will virtually disappear under closely knit steely grey and green foliage. Spreading rock plants, such as *Polygonum vacciniifolium*, *Dryas octopetala*, rock roses and thymes, can be inserted in the gaps. The adjacent beds are easily managed, planted with low perennials, small shrubs and dwarf bulbs and hardy cyclamen. A bold feature of flower and foliage is created with an urn on the lower terrace and the bird table near the centre of the garden provides another point of interest.

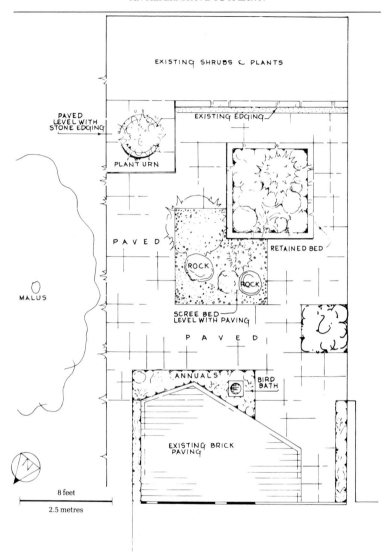

Plan 23: An alternative to a lawn, interrelating shingle and paving in a very small garden

Plan 23 depicts a previously characterless small site which has been improved by introducing an area of scree and different levels with paving and a raised rectangular bed. The area round the urn is about 6 inches (15 cm) high and the retained bed approximately 10 inches (25 cm) high. It could easily be adapted to include a larger section of shingle, with the paving reduced to

90

paths for walking across the garden. One or two well chosen rocks partly buried in the stones give a pleasing variation in texture and elevation, particularly if some carpeting plants are used around the base.

An alternative to the square bed would be a pool. This is best in sun, which most aquatic plants prefer, but if the water is in shade it should be kept chemically clear, with perhaps a fountain to ripple the surface. Hemerocallis, hosta and bergenia would be appropriate planted in the pebbles near the pool, although they will thrive equally in other parts of the garden.

A further combination of shingle and paving is illustrated in plan 24, which also incorporates a small lawn. The design focuses on the circle of bricks infilled with pebbles, and paving links the house to the workshop.

Apart from their aesthetic merits, pebbles are a relatively economical material and the labour involved is minimal. They are also very adaptable. In problem areas where the ground stays very wet in winter but dries up in summer, making weeds difficult to control, an attractive solution is to simulate an old river bed by strewing pebbles and boulders on the surface. There are many plants suitable for this situation, including *Cornus alba* 'Elegantissima', *C.alba* 'Spaethii', *Arundinaria nitida*, *A. murielae*, cultivars of *Miscanthus sinensis*, *Filipendula purpurea*, *Iris sibirica*, *I. foetidissima*, *Bergenia* hybrids and *Geranium macrorrhizum*. In shady places many ferns will tolerate a degree of dryness in summer, provided the roots are cool, and they look completely natural with fronds fanning out from under the larger rocks.

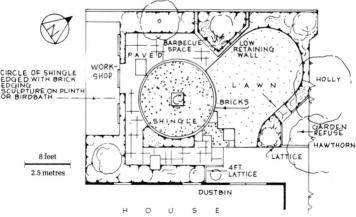

Plan 24: An alternative to a large lawn, with about two thirds of the garden under hard surfaces

A Herb Garden

Many of the old familiar flowers of our gardens could find a legitimate place in the herb garden. They were credited with curative, cosmetic and other powers in the past, recalled in common names like Cupid's dart and feverfew, and are not only of historical interest but often colourful and decorative plants. However, most people planning a herb garden today will concentrate on culinary herbs like thyme and parsley, perhaps adding a few others such as rue or balm for authenticity and effect. Grown in their own special area instead of relegated to a corner of the vegetable patch, herbs can become a delightful feature of the garden. Generally speaking, they thrive in any ordinary soil that is well drained but fairly moist and preferably in a light and sunny situation. It is sensible to keep mint, parsley, chives and others in everyday use within easy reach of the kitchen, but there is no reason why these should not be repeated in the herb garden itself.

The first requirements are to determine the amount of space available and to select the herbs one wishes to grow. There are various possible layouts. A circular garden with beds separated by paths radiating from the centre like the spokes of a cartwheel is attractive, but has the disadvantage that the narrow wedge-shaped sections offer very limited planting space. A rectangular design may be more practical. On a small scale, a simple method is to place paving stones 2 feet square (60 × 60 cm) with the corners just touching, forming a chequered pattern with alternate planting pockets, as illustrated in plan 25. The paving gives structural substance to the planting scheme, provides paths for walking among and picking the herbs and integrates the herb garden with the terrace or patio. Tall-growing fennel, tarragon and angelica would not be suitable for such a garden and are better grown elsewhere, perhaps in a mixed border with herbaceous plants, but many of the smaller herbs like chives, parsley and savory could be fitted into these compartments, together with a few pot marigolds for a touch of colour among the mauves, blues and whites.

A design on a larger scale is represented in plan 26 (overleaf), a herb garden measuring 60 × 46 feet (18 × 13.8 m), with room for a great variety of plants. This garden within a garden is completely enclosed except for the two gates, to create a feeling of seclusion and tranquillity and the illusion that we are taking a step back in

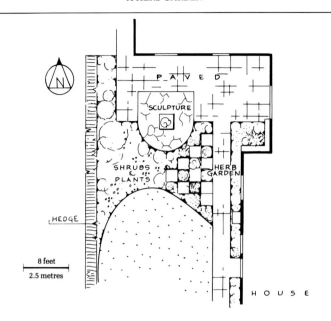

Plan 25: A herb garden incorporated in a small garden

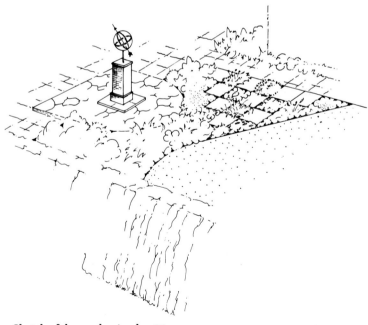

Sketch of the garden in plan 25

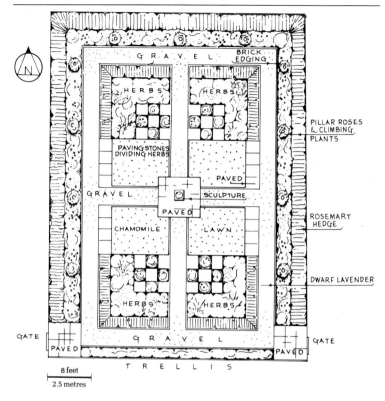

Plan 26: A herb garden as a self-contained entity

time. Hedges or trellis may be used, or a combination of the two, as shown on the plan. English yew, box or, on well drained soil, rosemary make good hedges, but trellis has much to recommend it, since it takes up less space and is not so time-consuming to maintain. It can also provide support for scented climbing plants and roses. The garden is large enough to contain a wide assortment of herbs. As well as the formal hedge of rosemary, dwarf lavender edges the four rectangular beds. The chequerboard pattern is made up as before, with five paving stones and four compartments for small plants. Taller herbs could be grown in the four L-shaped borders and need not be restricted purely to culinary sorts.

Above: A herb garden at the Chelsea Show, 1986, with compartments formed by bricks and concrete slabs

Below: A herb garden divided by hedges of dwarf box and enclosed with climbing roses

The old-fashioned *Monarda didyma*, flowering from summer to autumn, is attractive to bees

The list below is a selection of plants that qualify for a place in the herb garden because of their historical associations and ornamental value. Culinary herbs are dealt with in the Wisley Handbook of that title.

Achillea millefolium (yarrow, milfoil) has been cultivated for medicinal purposes since the fifteenth century and is best in the red and pink forms; 2 feet (60 cm) high.
Anthemis nobilis (chamomile) was valued from very early times as a tonic and a cure for fever. In Tudor days it was popular for lawns.

Artemisia abrotanum (southernwood, old man, lad's love) has been recognized for its curative properties since the first century. The odour from the leaves is reputed to keep away moths, hence the intriguing French name *garde-robe* (literally wardrobe); 3 to 4 feet (90–120 cm) high.

Campanula persicifolia (peach-leafed bellflower) was an ingredient in several remedies and is very decorative with its blue flowers; 3 feet (90 cm) high.

Catananche caerulea (Cupid's dart) was formerly used in love potions and has blue flowers; 2 feet (60 cm) high.

Chrysanthemum parthenium (feverfew) has enjoyed a recent revival for its medicinal qualities, particularly the treatment of migraine, and the golden-leafed form, 'Aureum', is an excellent foliage plant with white flowers; 2 feet (60 cm) high.

Eryngium maritimum (sea holly) grows wild on our sea shores and the roots and leaves were supposed to heal many different ailments. It has attractive steely blue thistle-like flowers; 2 feet (60 cm) high.

Monarda didyma (scarlet bergamot, Oswego tea, bee balm) has scented leaves which were used for tea and brilliant scarlet flowers, showy enough to include in any planting scheme; 4 feet (1.2 m) high.

Origanum majorana (sweet majoram) was much esteemed by the ancient Greeks and has been grown in England since the fourteenth century; a well known culinary herb, it is also worth a place for its pretty sprays of mauve flowers; 2 feet (60 cm) high.

Pulmonaria officinalis (lungwort, soldiers and sailors, Jerusalem cowslip, spotted dog) was used as a pot herb in the past and believed to have numerous medicinal qualities. It has large silver-spotted leaves and pink flowers changing to blue; 6 to 9 inches (15–22 cm) high.

Tanacetum vulgare (tansy) was employed as a bitter flavouring, especially in tansy pudding, and as a remedy for various complaints. It has yellow flowers; 2 to 3 feet (60–90 cm) high.

Viola tricolor (heart's ease), our native wild pansy, has many other common names and was once considered to have excellent curative properties. Growing at random among larger plants in beds and between paving, it is most attractive and produces its purple, yellow and white or blue flowers over a long period; 3 inches (7 cm) high.

A Period Garden

At the beginning of the eighteenth century when Queen Anne came to the throne, the English formal garden was at its peak and the landscape movement, which would sweep away the enclosed spaces and intricate patterns of the Tudors and Stuarts, had scarcely begun. The repertoire of garden plants had also expanded and many new introductions were by then established in cultivation.

Probably introduced by the Crusaders, *Lychnis chalcedonica* does best in a sunny position (see p. 100)

A period garden of this kind is not difficult for the modern gardener to reproduce and it is a fascinating exercise for anyone interested in the evolution of gardening and the history of plants. Plan 27 is a simplified design for an imaginary garden of about 1700, containing authentic plants which would have been in cultivation at that date. Many of these are still grown unchanged today and are readily available, although others have been replaced by more recent hybrids. The planting scheme is intended to distribute specific areas of colour in different parts of the garden. (See overleaf for key to plants numbered on the plan.)

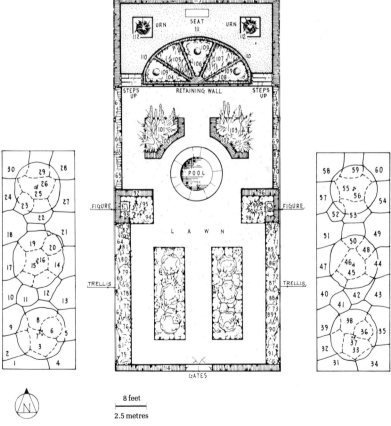

Plan 27: A period garden, with seventeenth-century plants

Key

Island beds

1	7	*Dianthus barbatus* (sweet William)
2	5	*Pulsatilla vulgaris* (*Anemone pulsatilla*) (pasque flower)
3	5	*Gladiolus illyricus*
4	5	*Impatiens balsamina* (balsam, touch-me-not) – summer
	15	*Narcissus* × *incomparabilis* – spring
5	5	*Dictamnus albus* (*D. fraxinella*) (burning bush)
6	3	*Lychnis chalcedonica* (Maltese or Jerusalem cross)
7	1	*Rosa gallica* 'Versicolor' ('Rosa Mundi')
8	3	*Saponaria officinalis* 'Albo Plena', 'Roseo Plena', 'Rubra Plena' (soapwort)
9	5	*Impatiens balsamina* – summer
	15	*Narcissus* × *incomparabilis* – spring
10	5	*Lychnis coronaria* (rose campion, dusty miller)
11	3	*Lilium martagon* (Turk's cap lily)
12	3	*Verbascum nigrum* (dark mullein)
13	5	*Impatiens balsamina* – summer
	15	*Narcissus* × *incomparabilis* – spring
14	3	*Centaurea montana* (cornflower, mountain knapweed)
15	3	*Geranium pratense* (cranesbill)
16	1	*Rosa* × *alba* (white rose)
17	3	*Tradescantia virginiana* (spiderwort)
18	5	*Impatiens balsamina* – summer
	15	*Narcissus* × *incomparabilis* – spring
19	3	*Hemerocallis flava* (daylily)
20	3	*Lilium candidum* (Madonna lily)
21	5	*Aquilegia vulgaris* (columbine)
22	3	*Asphodeline lutea* (asphodel, king's spear)
23	3	*Lychnis chalcedonica*
24	7	*Dianthus barbatus*
25	1	*Rosa gallica officinalis* (apothecaries' rose, red rose of Lancaster)
26	3	*Polemonium caeruleum* (Jacob's ladder) (see p. 103)
27	5	*Impatiens balsamina* – summer
	15	*Narcissus* × *incomparabilis* – spring
28	5	*Geum rivale* (water avens)
29	5	*Dianthus plumarius* (pink)
30	3	*Campanula glomerata* (bellflower)
31	5	*Aquilegia vulgaris*
32	9	*Linum arboreum* (tree flax)
33	3	*Polygonatum multiflorum* (Solomon's seal)
34	3	*Eryngium planum* (sea holly)
35	3	*Thalictrum minus* (*T. adiantifolium*) (meadow rue)
36	3	*Lilium candidum*
37	1	*Rosa gallica officinalis*
38	3	*Campanula trachelium* (throatwort)
39	5	*Impatiens balsamina* – summer
	15	*Narcissus* × *incomparabilis* – spring

40	3	*Centaurea montana*
41	3	*Lysimachia vulgaris* (yellow loosestrife)
42	3	*Agrimonia eupatoria* (agrimony)
43	5	*Impatiens balsamina* – summer
	15	*Narcissus × incomparabilis* – spring
44	3	*Origanum onites* (pot majoram)
45	5	*Gladiolus illyricus*
46	1	*Rosa × alba*
47	3	*Tradescantia virginiana*
48	3	*Lychnis chalcedonica*
49	3	*Centranthus ruber* (red valerian)
50	3	*Chelidonium majus* 'Flore Pleno' (greater celandine)
51	5	*Impatiens balsamina* – summer
	15	*Narcissus × incomparabilis* – spring
52	3	*Lilium candidum*
53	3	*Tanacetum vulgare* (tansy)
54	5	*Impatiens balsamina* – summer
	15	*Narcissus × incomparabilis* – spring
55	5	*Gladiolus illyricus*
56	1	*Rosa gallica* 'Versicolor'
57	1	*Aster amellus*
58	3	*Pulmonaria officinalis* (lungwort)
59	3	*Chrysanthemum parthenium* 'Aureum' (feverfew)
60	7	*Dianthus barbatus*

Planting scheme for garden layout

61	1	*Rosmarinus officinalis* (rosemary)
62	1	*Jasminum officinale* (jasmine)
63	1	*Rosmarinus officinalis*
64	1	*Clematis flammula*
65	1	*Lonicera periclymenum* (honeysuckle, woodbine)
66	1	*Rosmarinus officinalis*
67	1	*Lathyrus latifolius* (perennial pea)
68	1	*Clematis flammula*
69	1	*Rosmarinus officinalis*
70	1	*Jasminum officinale*
71	1	*Lathyrus latifolius*
72	1	*Rosmarinus officinalis*
73	1	*Lonicera periclymenum*
74	1	*Rosmarinus officinalis*
75	7	*Astrantia major* (black masterwort)
76	5	*Lilium bulbiferum croceum* (orange lily)
77	5	*Alchemilla vulgaris* (lady's mantle)
78	5	*Lilium bulbiferum croceum*
79	5	*Alchemilla vulgaris*
80	5	*Lilium bulbiferum croceum*
81	5	*Alchemilla vulgaris*
82	3	*Althaea rosea* (hollyhock)
83	25	*Lavandula angustifolia* (*L. spica*) (English lavender)
84	3	*Althaea rosea*

85	5	*Alchemilla vulgaris*
86	5	*Lilium bulbiferum croceum*
87	5	*Alchemilla vulgaris*
88	5	*Lilium bulbiferum croceum*
89	5	*Alchemilla vulgaris*
90	5	*Lilium bulbiferum croceum*
91	7	*Astrantia major*
92	14	*Phillyrea latifolia spinosa*
93	12	*Convallaria majalis* (lily-of-the-valley)
94	9	*Lamium maculatum* (spotted dead nettle)
95	1	*Yucca filamentosa* (silk grass)
96	14	*Phillyrea latifolia spinosa*
97	12	*Convallaria majalis*
98	9	*Lamium maculatum*
99	1	*Yucca filamentosa*
100	14	*Phillyrea latifolia spinosa*
101	5	*Acanthus mollis* (bear's breeches)
102	14	*Phillyrea latifolia spinosa*
103	5	*Acanthus mollis*
104	15	*Armeria maritima* (thrift)
105	6	*Canna indica* (Indian shot) – summer
	50	tulips striped or feathered – spring
106	15	*Armeria maritima*
107	6	*Canna indica* – summer
	50	tulips striped or feathered – spring
108	15	*Armeria maritima*
109	3	*Kochia scoparia trichophylla* (summer cypress)
110	120 feet (36.5 m)	*Buxus sempervirens* 'Suffruticosa' (edging box)
111	30	*Anthemis nobilis* (camomile)
112	3	*Agave americana marginata* (American aloe)
	24	*Hyacinthus orientalis* (hyacinth)
113	60	*Taxus baccata* (English yew)
114	30	*Taxus baccata*

Interplanting for island beds in vacant spaces

Lysimachia nummularia (creeping Jenny, moneywort)
Viola tricolor (heart's ease)
Meconopsis cambrica (Welsh poppy)
Hieracium aurantiacum (orange hawkweed)
Geranium phaeum (mourning widow)
Iberis umbellata (candytuft) – seed

Above: *Polemonium caeruleum*, contributing a cool blue in early summer, has been grown since Roman times

Below: *Meconopsis cambrica*, a native of Britain, produces its brilliant flowers in late spring

The landscape movement which became so fashionable in the eighteenth century was based on the principle that the garden should merge with the surrounding countryside to form a single panoramic picture, including perhaps a man-made lake, a Grecian temple, groups of trees nestling in the folds of distant hills and livestock grazing near the house without any visible boundary fence. The picture was, of course, an illusion brought about by the ha-ha, a broad steep ditch which does not impede the view.

However, the use of the ha-ha need not be confined to large estates such as those created by Lancelot 'Capability' Brown. It can be extremely effective in a garden of moderate size in a space only about 40 feet (12 m) wide. The first consideration is drainage, which will be influenced by the texture of the soil and the lie of the land, and there should be adequate provision for piping away any

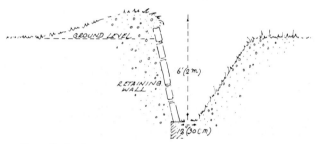

Cross-section of a ha-ha

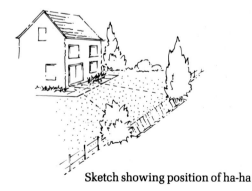

Sketch showing position of ha-ha

Above: A ha-ha viewed from the 'visible' side, with the retaining wall

Below: *Osmanthus × burkwoodii*, a useful hardy evergreen shrub with fragrant flowers in April and May (see p. 106)

water that might collect in the bottom of the trench. Originally, when labour and materials were cheap, a ha-ha might be dug as deep as 8 feet (2.4 m), but 5 to 6 feet (1.5–1.8 m) should be sufficient, depending on the animals to be kept in the pasture (see figure, p. 104). The flat bottom of the trench should be 1 foot (30 cm) wide and a retaining wall should be built up the steeper side, ensuring that holes are made towards the base for drainage. This wall can be constructed of bricks or stone or old railway sleepers, although the latter are not very attractive. Concrete walling blocks are relatively inexpensive and weather quickly, becoming covered with moss and lichen on a north-facing surface. The bank opposite the wall should be turfed.

It is a great help if the ha-ha can be placed where the land falls away from the viewpoint towards the open country. One can then dig into the slope and spread surplus soil over the higher ground in front of the ha-ha to raise the height of the wall. Groups of evergreen shrubs and medium-sized conifers planted at each end of the ha-ha will frame the view. Suitable shrubs would be *Osmanthus* × *burkwoodii, Stranvaesia davidiana, Cotoneaster lacteus, C.* 'Cornubia', *Elaeagnus* × *ebbingei* and *Viburnum rhytidophyllum*. It goes without saying that the lawn should flow towards the top of the wall of the ha-ha without interruption.

A sunken fence is another way to achieve an invisible boundary and requires less excavation (see below). A trench is dug 4 feet (1.2 m) deep with sloping sides. The width should be 10 feet (3 m) at the top and 3 feet (90 cm) at the bottom and a post-and-wire fence is erected along the middle of the trench below eye-level.

A sunken fence

A Heather Garden

One could probably say without exaggeration that heathers contribute more colour throughout the year than any other group of plants and the relatively short gap between the end of April and the end of June, when they are not in flower, is bridged by those with golden or bronze foliage. Most heathers require a lime-free soil, although *Erica herbacea* (*E. carnea*) and *E.* × *darleyensis* are happy enough except on very thin chalky soils, giving us some of the best winter colour from November to April (see also the Wisley Handbook, *Heaths and Heathers*).

There are several ways to make a heather garden, one of the deciding factors being the space available. However, even a few square yards is sufficient for a varied collection interplanted with dwarf conifers. Whether planting in hundreds or in small numbers, rewarding results can be expected for very little work. The beautiful heather gardens at Kew, Edinburgh and the RHS Garden, Wisley, are laid out on a grander scale than most of us could imagine in our own gardens, but much can be learned from the principles on which they are designed. Heathers should be planted 1 to 1¼ feet (30–37 cm) apart, in groups of at least three to five of the same sort; single plants are never effective. These drifts can be allowed to overlap where they meet for a less contrived appearance.

Unless one is prepared to do some propagating from a small nucleus of plants, even a modest heather garden can be costly to stock. Fortunately, heathers are fairly easy to raise from cuttings and will develop into good flowering plants within little more than a year. Another economical method is to reduce the number of heathers by choosing suitable conifers and shrubs to complement them and fill up spaces in the beds. *Juniperus communis* 'Repanda', which makes a green rug-like carpet, and *J. communis* 'Hornibrookii', with grey-green foliage spreading in all directions to follow the contours of the ground, can both be recommended. They will cover an area 10 to 12 feet (3–3.6 m) across – equivalent to about 50 heathers. *Cotoneaster dammeri*, an evergreen shrub with red berries, is completely prostrate and extends indefinitely over the ground, though it is easily controlled. *Rubus calycinoides* forms dense widespreading mats of evergreen glossy leaves with white flowers.

A new heather garden often looks bare and sparsely planted

Left: A small bed of heathers and dwarf conifers against a background of shrubs

Right: The leaves and flowers of *Anaphalis triplinervis* 'Summer Snow' make an attractive foil for heathers

---

before the heathers and shrubs have grown together and become established. One solution is to cover the soil with a layer of moist coarse peat or forest bark, which provides an attractive foil for the plants. However, it must be emphasized that the mulch and the soil should be thoroughly moist before application, otherwise the shrubs might suffer from lack of water.

A place for *Hamamelis mollis* should be found in the heather garden. With its bright yellow flowers and upright branches, it is an ideal shrub for underplanting with *Erica herbacea* 'King George' ('Winter Beauty'), to provide one of the finest examples of winter colour from December to February. (See also *Heaths and Heathers* for further suggestions of shrub and conifers to use with heathers.)

The planting schemes illustrated in plan 28 are for island beds, but they can be adapted to fit in with other shapes and with the overall design of the garden concerned. If the beds are divided by grass paths, for instance, some of the plants can be repeated on each side.

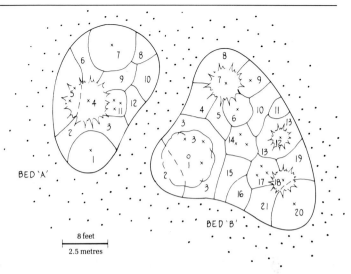

BED 'A'

8 feet

2.5 metres

BED 'B'

Plan 28: A heather garden, with shrubs and groundcover

Key
Bed A

1	1	*Juniperus communis* 'Repanda'
2	9	*Calluna vulgaris* 'Tib'
3	10	*Erica herbacea* 'King George' ('Winter Beauty')
4	1	*Chamaecyparis pisifera* 'Filifera Aurea'
5	2	*Rubus calycinoides*
6	9	*Erica vagans* 'Mrs D. F. Maxwell'
7	1	*Erica arborea alpina*
8	5	*Erica herbacea* 'King George'
9	9	*Calluna vulgaris* 'Alportii'
10	5	*Stachys* 'Silver Carpet'
11	3	*Helictotrichon sempervirens*
12	7	*Erica vagans* 'Mrs D. F. Maxwell'

Bed B

1	1	*Hamamelis mollis*
2	10	*Erica herbacea* 'King George'
3	3	*Cotoneaster dammeri*

4	7	*Calluna vulgaris* 'Mair's Variety'
5	7	*Calluna vulgaris* 'J. H. Hamilton'
6	1	*Cistus* 'Silver Pink'
7	1	*Chamaecyparis pisifera* 'Boulevard'
8	7	*Polygonum vacciniifolium*
9	1	*Juniperus sabina* 'Tamariscifolia'
10	9	*Calluna vulgaris* 'Peter Sparkes'
11	3	*Anaphalis triplinervis*
12	1	*Thuja orientalis* 'Aurea Nana'
13	15	*Erica herbacea* 'King George'
14	3	*Ceratostigma willmottianum*
15	9	*Erica × darleyensis*
16	5	*Calluna vulgaris* 'Golden Feather'
17	3	*Helictotrichon sempervirens*
18	1	*Chamaecyparis lawsoniana* 'Ellwoodii'
19	12	*Erica vagans* 'St Keverne'
20	1	*Genista lydia*

The colour of the garden furniture is echoed in the glaucous foliage of rue. In the foreground, acanthus spikes rise up

Gardens of Different Shapes and Sizes

TWO NARROW GARDENS MERGED IN ONE

In plan 13(p. 114)two narrow adjoining gardens are united in one, the plot on the right being 1 foot (30 cm) lower than the other. The split in levels contributes useful features to the design, necessitating a limited amount of structural stonework, with steps leading down from the new pergola and sufficient walling to make a flat area for the patio and a small lawn. Elsewhere the different levels are absorbed into the borders adjacent to the path.

The outline of the garden invites a way of approach from various directions. The position of the pergola is governed by an existing grapevine and fortuitously allows it to be placed at an angle.

A MEDIUM-SIZED GARDEN OF UNUSUAL SHAPE

Plan 30 (p. 115) demonstrates different requirements in a triangular garden of medium size. It includes a naturalized area and small hazel coppice, a summerhouse, beds for shrub roses, herbaceous perennials and dahlias, flowering and berrying shrubs, a rock garden, a plot for vegetables and fruit and a greenhouse.

The garden was originally planted many years ago and inferior shrubs and trees have been discarded. The ones specified on the plan were considered to contribute to the reconstruction of the garden.

A GREENHOUSE AS A FEATURE

The hexagonal greenhouse can be an attractive feature in its own right, but is even better if integrated with the design of the garden.

Overleaf above: A rock garden planted with undemanding alpines, including aubrieta, saxifrage and iberis

Below: An alternative to the rectangular lawn, flanked by mixed borders and rising to a pool at the end

Page 113 above: Imaginative use of crazy paving in curves and steps

Below: Paving is a feature of many gardens, old and new, and can be very decorative

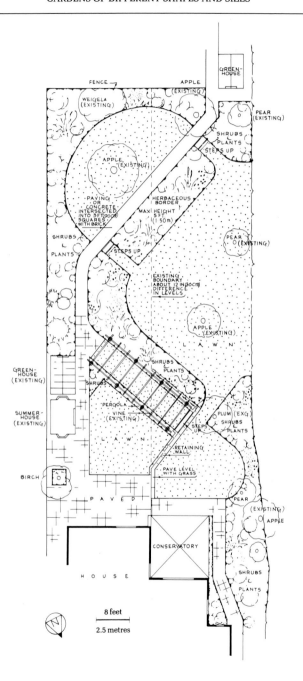

8 feet

2.5 metres

Plan 29: Two narrow gardens in one

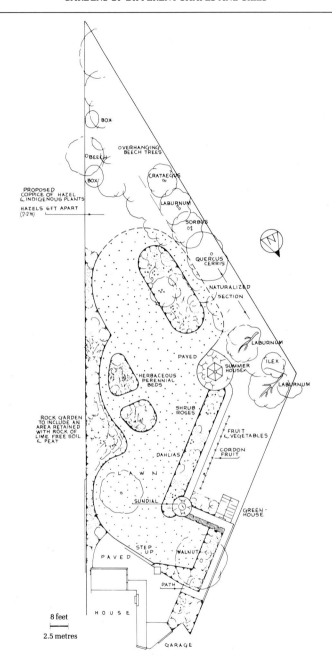

BOX

OVERHANGING
BEECH TREES

BEECH

BOX

CRATAEGUS

PROPOSED
COPPICE OF HAZEL
& INDIGENOUS PLANTS

HAZELS 6FT APART
(2·2m)

LABURNUM

SORBUS

QUERCUS
CERRIS

N

NATURALIZED
SECTION

LABURNUM

ILEX

PAVED

SUMMER
HOUSE

HERBACEOUS
PERENNIAL
BEDS

LABURNUM

SHRUB
ROSES

ROCK GARDEN
TO INCLUDE AN
AREA RETAINED
WITH ROCK OF
LIME FREE SOIL
& PEAT

FRUIT
& VEGETABLES

CORDON
FRUIT

DAHLIAS

L A W N

SUNDIAL

GREEN-
HOUSE

STEP
UP

WALNUT

PAVED

PATH

8 feet

2.5 metres

H O U S E

G A R A G E

Plan 30: A medium-sized garden of unusual shape

115

Plan 31: A garden including a greenhouse

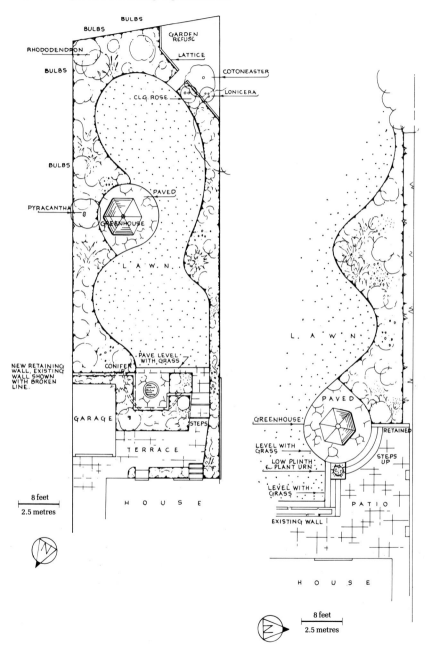

Plan 32: A patio with a greenhouse

In this respect plans **31** and **32** are basically similar. One shows a complete garden with existing trees and shrubs and the other illustrates a corner of a garden specifically intended to combine the greenhouse with the planting scheme and patio. In both cases, the area surrounding the greenhouse has been laid out in a similar manner, except the reverse way round.

A VERY SMALL GARDEN INCORPORATING A LAWN

The garden in plan **33** measures less than 48 feet (14.4m) by 18 feet (5.4m) and the intention is to introduce a design that is an alternative to a rectangular lawn, bordered by a narrow bed.

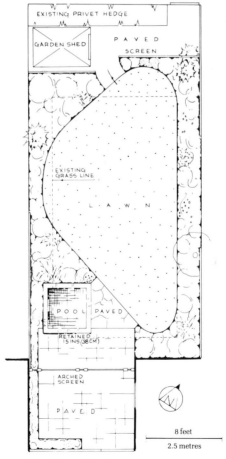

Plan 33: A very small garden with a lawn

or what might be described as a lawn with a fringe. It is an example of how a lawn can be included satisfactorily in a very small space and again outlines should be continuous and not broken up with little curves. The raised pool is situated near the house and aquatic plants and active life in and over the water can be seen at first hand from the house and on the patio.

INTRODUCING CURVES TO ADD SPACE

Curves in a small garden 60 by 34 feet (18 by 10.2 m) increase the visual impression that the garden is larger than it really is. In plan 34 the line of paving and of the beds flows without interruption and there are two focal points – the urn on the left and a small conifer on the right at the widest point of the border, which balances a view of the ornamental tree on the lawn.

There is a choice of material for the patio. Crazy paving can be fitted easily into a curve, but is a little more difficult to lay than reconstituted stone, which is made in fixed sizes and thicknesses and can be cut to the required shape with a masonry saw.

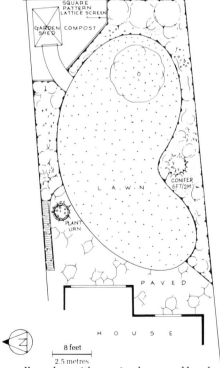

Plan 34: A small garden with curving lawn and borders

CREATING VISTAS

The layout of the garden in plan 35 creates unimpeded views by using the maximum amount of space available. The major emphasis lies towards the right, with the bird bath and conifer on each side of a broad grass inlet. The circle of bricks is centralized

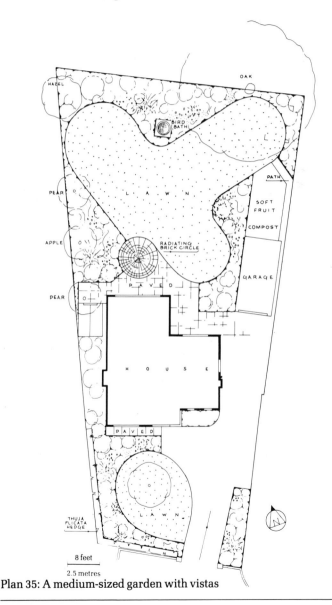

Plan 35: A medium-sized garden with vistas

on the door to the garden and makes an attractive contrast to the shape and colour of the patio. It could equally well be constructed with concrete setts, which adapt so easily to form curved patterns and circles.

The garage intrudes into the garden, but the three directional design detracts from its presence. At the front of the house, the lawn has an unbroken outline to complement a small specimen tree and is flanked by shrubs providing interest and colour throughout the year. Shrubs and trees planted by the previous owners are shown on the plan.

Above: Roses and honeysuckle cover a pergola. Blue flower spikes of delphiniums look particularly attractive with pink roses

Opposite: Conifers and heathers combine to form an attractive, low-maintenance garden

Trees for
Small Gardens

⎯ KEITH RUSHFORTH ⎯

Pink *Tamarisk*, yellow *Laburnum* and white lilac, *Syringa*, are
seen here with rosemary and *Bergenia*

Introduction

Trees are essential to any garden, contributing a beauty and a presence which no other plant or feature can provide. They fill a host of roles, giving scale and a framework to the surroundings, shade on hot summer afternoons, a colourful display of flower, fruit, foliage or bark. Trees are needed whatever the size and shape of the garden. However, small gardens demand extra care and thought in the use, choice and location of trees. The object of this book is to assist in the selection, planting, pruning and management, and simply the enjoyment, of trees in small gardens.

A dictionary definition of a tree is 'a perennial woody plant with an evident trunk', which is somewhat vague. The tallest tree in the world, a coastal redwood, *Sequoia sempervirens*, is as tall as the dome of St Paul's Cathedral at 364 ft (111 m), yet most trees are very much smaller. The term 'tree' is used here to include all woody plants which have, or can be trained to have, a single stem and will grow more than 13 ft (4 m) tall. Several very useful 'trees' for small gardens might be termed large shrubs in larger spaces.

A small garden may range in size from the back garden typical of new housing estates, only about 20 by 30 ft (6 by 9 m), to one measuring some 50 by 70 ft (15 by 21 m). Even in the smallest space, trees are necessary to bring out the best of the garden. In a larger area, the requirement is often not for larger trees, but for more trees, or for trees used to create a series of intimate rooms.

The tightly clustered, bright red berries of *Sorbus scalaris*, ripening in October, are set off by fronds of glossy leaves

125

The Value of Trees in a Small Garden

Choosing a tree just because you like it or its description may achieve a satisfactory result but is unlikely to maximize the potential of the garden. This chapter aims to give general guidance on the selection of trees for a small garden, taking account of their attributes, such as shape and scale, leaves and flowers, screening and support, and relating these to the overall scheme. (For detailed information on individual trees, see pp.152–176.)

SCALE

One of the beauties of a tree is that it is usually the largest object in the garden. However, a tree which is several times taller than everything else will often be totally out of proportion and, instead of enhancing a situation, may dominate it. It is important therefore to consider not just the physical size of the tree but its scale in relation to its surroundings and to other features of the garden.

Shape is equally relevant. A tall narrow shape can be used to punctuate a view or to lead the eye skywards and will be in keeping with high buildings. Examples range from the obelisks of certain very compactly upright or fastigiate forms, such as *Prunus* 'Amanogawa' and *Chamaecyparis lawsoniana* 'Columnaris', to more loosely upright trees like *Sorbus rehderiana* 'Joseph Rock'. A widespreading tree, however, will be more appropriate in a low and sprawling setting, although there are occasions when a discordant element can be useful, perhaps to accentuate the predominant features of the site. Among spreading trees with arching branches are *Sorbus scalaris* and *Acer davidii*. Those with a weeping habit, such as *Pyrus salicifolia* 'Pendula' and *Alnus incana* 'Pendula' can be used to form tumbling fountains of foliage.

A tree must also relate to space within the garden and should not be overbearing where this is limited, as in a small garden. A tree will generally be too large if it is taller or broader than the open space in front of it. As a rough guide, the tree should be from half to two thirds as tall and wide as the length and breadth of the entire garden. For instance, in a garden 33 ft (10 m) long and 20 ft (6 m) wide, a tree 16 to 23 ft (5–7 m) tall with a spread of around 13 ft (4 m) planted at one end should be in scale both with the space and with the lawn of 16 by 23 ft (5 by 7 m). However, trees which are either very narrow and tall or very broad and low can safely exceed this figure, so long as they are in harmony with other aspects of the site, without becoming too imposing.

SHADE

The shade of a tree can be welcome on a hot summer day and a nuisance at other times. All trees cast shade, which is an important factor to remember before planting them, and their shape and location should be considered in relation to the position of the sun and the times of day when the garden, or sun on the house, will be most appreciated. The density of shade, which is determined by the way the leaves fit together, should also be taken into account. Trees with small or pinnate leaves (where the leaf is composed of a number of small leaflets), like birch or rowan, cast light shade, while trees with large leaves, such as whitebeam, cast a heavier shade. However, this is not absolute and holly, which has small closely set leaves, casts a thick shade.

The density of shade will affect the use of the ground beneath. Deep shade may give a cool spot for sitting out in a hot summer but could be disastrous if you wish to grow plants there. Lighter, more dappled shade is needed for the purpose, provided by trees such as oak which are deep rooting and do not cause severe root competition with other plants. This sort of shade is particularly suitable for rhododendrons and other woodland plants. If shade is required over a patio or terrace, avoid trees like *Prunus*, *Acer* and *Tilia*, which are liable to become infested with aphids producing sticky honeydew. It is also wise to choose trees which are in full leaf by the beginning of May – in the British climate the one hot day of the year is just as likely to be then as in August!

FOLIAGE, FLOWERS, FRUIT AND BARK

Apart from being attractive in themselves, the foliage, flowers, fruit or bark of a tree will influence its appearance within the garden and in turn alter the perceived scale. For instance, large leaves, flowers or fruits tend to be more visible and thus make a space seem smaller. They are useful for achieving an effect of enclosed intimacy or for shortening a long vista, perhaps in a narrow garden, but can be claustrophobic in a pocket-sized plot. Here, trees with small leaves, flowers or fruits, or large leaves composed of many small leaflets, can be recommended, to emphasize space and make the small seem bigger. To take two examples from a single genus, *Sorbus* – *S. thibetica* 'John Mitchell' with its large simple leaves will create a feeling of smallness and closeness, whereas the feathery foliage of S. *vilmorinii*, with many small leaflets, will give the illusion of distance and expansiveness.

Leaves. The leaves are the most numerous and prominent components of a tree. Their green colour is due to chlorophyll, which converts the energy in sunlight to manufacture sugars, and there are usually other pigments present which can also absorb sunlight to carry out photosynthesis. When these are plentiful, as in many forms of the popular Japanese maple, *Acer palmatum*, they lead to purple, red, gold, or yellow foliage. The proportions of the two groups of compounds may change as the foliage matures, so the leaves emerge in one colour and take on a different hue later. For instance, *Aesculus neglecta* 'Erythroblastos' has pink young leaves which turn pale green and the bluish green foliage of *Pinus sylvestris* 'Aurea' becomes light gold in winter.

Leaves may also have a silvery or grey appearance, caused by hairs reflecting the light, as in *Pyrus salicifolia* 'Pendula', or by a waxy covering which prevents water loss, as in conifers like *Abies koreana*.

Variegated leaves, in which two or more colours are mixed together – frequently white or cream with green – are usually the result of some physiological oddity in the plant. Many variegated plants revert and produce shoots with plain green leaves, which must be removed in order to maintain the effect.

Leaves are deciduous, if they are lost each year in the autumn; or evergreen, in which case they are lost at various times of the year, so that the tree is never leafless; or semi-evergreen, when they are normally evergreen and lost only in severe winters or just before the new leaves grow. Many deciduous plants display bold and attractive autumn colours on the dying leaves.

Flowers. Compared to the foliage, the flowers of a tree are a temporary feature and often of rather short duration, but they can be very decorative when open. If borne before the leaves unfold in the spring, such as those of *Magnolia kobus* or the catkins of the goat willow, *Salix caprea*, they are particularly striking. Other trees carry the flowers with the developing leaves, like *Prunus* 'Umineko', or later in the summer, like *Cornus kousa*, or even in the autumn, like *Ligustrum lucidum*. It is possible to choose trees

---

With its drooping branches and silvery willow-like leaves, *Pyrus salicifolia* 'Pendula' is the most ornamental of the pears

Above left: 'Lutescens', a cultivar of the native whitebeam, *Sorbus aria*; the silvery effect of the foliage helps to compensate for the shade which it casts

Above right: The popular *Acer negundo* 'Variegatum' is particularly effective when hung with winged fruits, but is inclined to lose its variegation

Below left: *Magnolia* × *loebneri* 'Leonard Messel', a hybrid of *M. kobus*, bears purplish pink flowers in April, before the leaves appear

Below right: Sometimes known as the coral bark maple from the strikingly coloured young stems, *Acer palmatum* 'Senkaki' also has delicate yellow green leaves

Opposite: *Robinia pseudoacacia* 'Frisia', with feathery golden yellow foliage in summer, is a fine specimen tree for a town garden

to bloom in succession from February to November, although the majority flower in spring. A number of them, including cherries, crab apples and mahonias, have the bonus of a pleasant scent.

Fruit. Trees normally ripen their fruits in autumn, although many *Prunus* do so in early summer. There are numerous trees which may be grown for the beauty of their fruits, notably rowans, whitebeams and hollies, and also of course for eating. (Fruit trees as such are not covered in this book; see *The Fruit Garden Displayed* for details of these).

Bark and twigs. Some trees are valuable for their ornamental barks or twigs, often most apparent in winter when the twigs have ripened to their distinctive colours and the leaves have been shed. The winter twigs of *Acer palmatum* 'Senkaki' are coral-red, while those of several willows are covered with a greyish green waxy bloom. The snow gum, *Eucalyptus niphophila*, and a number of birches have white barks and the paperbark maple, *Acer griseum*, has a flaking bark of rich reddish brown.

SCREENING

Apart from their own beauty, many trees have a screening function in gardens, visually separating two areas. It is important to decide what sort of screen is required. Too often, trees which grow to 100 ft (30 m) tall are planted where a height of 20 ft (6 m) would be sufficient, perhaps between the bedroom windows of neighbouring two-storey houses. The ubiquitous Leyland cypress, × *Cupressocyparis leylandii*, is a notorious offender. A screen between ground-floor windows should only be 10 ft (3 m) high and, between one ground-floor window and a neighbouring first floor one, 15 ft (4.5 m). Planting tall-growing trees in these situations is a recipe for heavy shade, general aggravation and unnecessary work. Choose trees which fit the bill, like common holly or the Lawson cypress, even if they take one or more years to reach the desired height, and forget about Leyland cypress – it has no place in a small garden.

Sometimes, deciduous trees can be as effective for screening as evergreens, with the winter tracery of the branches preventing through vision and leading the eye away. They are useful too if the screening is needed only during the summer, for instance, to provide privacy for sunbathing. Hawthorn, whitebeam or even hazel might be good choices.

SUPPORT FOR CLIMBERS

Any tree or large shrub can be used as a support for climbing plants, such as *Clematis montana*, variegated ivy, *Rosa filipes* 'Toby Tristram' or *Wisteria sinensis*. This is a good way to grow large climbers which do not sit well on a trellis, so long as they are not prone to diseases and do not need pampering with pruning to produce flowers. It can also be applied to fruit trees where the fruit crop is superfluous, although if you wish to pick most of the fruit, I recommend a non-prickly climber.

SHELTER FOR WILDLIFE

Trees inevitably attract birds and other wildlife to a garden, adding yet another dimension to the pleasure derived from them. They provide shelter in winter, especially conifers, nesting places in spring and food in the form of fruits, seeds or foliage-eating insects.

The Tibetan cherry, *Prunus serrula*, a vigorous small tree valued for the polished bark

Practical Considerations

POSITIONING TREES

Trees should be placed where they can be seen to best advantage. Generally, and especially in a restricted space, a tree looks better if it is at the end of an open expanse rather than in the centre. In a front or back garden, this would be near the boundary.

Boundaries. However, a tree must never be positioned directly on a boundary, as this can cause problems when the crown or system of branches develops on the far side. If someone is harmed by a tree overhanging the pavement from your garden, you may be liable for damages. Similarly, your neighbour has the right to remove any branches intruding into his or her garden and may cut them back to the boundary, but no further. The offending material is technically trespassing, although it remains the property of the owner, to whom it should be given back, and cannot be used without permission. Thus to pick overhanging fruit is theft.

Finally, do not place a tree immediately in front of a window but to the side, which is much better in the long term.

Foundations and drains. There are other possible disadvantages of having trees in a garden, apart from shade and root competition with other plants, which should be considered before planting. If the roots of a tree grow beneath the footings of a wall, they can lift or 'jack-up' the wall as they expand, and lead to cracking. This often happens to low walls with very scanty foundations, but rarely to a house. The remedy is to plant the tree some distance from the wall. With small trees, there is little risk if they are kept at least 3 ft (1 m) away.

Some trees, especially willows, can grow in a drain and block it. However, this does not occur unless the drain is already fractured or the joints are poor and it is rarely serious. When planting over or near the run of a weak drain, a precaution would be to choose a tree which is not likely to grow in such wet conditions and prefers dry sandy soils.

In extreme cases, trees may cause subsidence of the foundations of a house. However, this only happens during a dry summer on certain clay subsoils, which shrink as they dry out, and is more of a problem in areas of low rainfall, including southeast England. Provided the house has adequate foundations, small trees can usually be safely planted at a distance of 16 ft (5 m) from them. If you are concerned, advice should be sought either from your local authority or from a qualified arboricultural consultant.

Ultimate size. Trees do not conveniently reach a given size and then cease, for while they live, they grow. However, as they approach maturity and start to flower and fruit profusely, they will slow down, most small trees eventually growing only 2 to 6 in. (5–15 cm) a year in height and radius. The smaller the estimated maximum height of the tree, the slower it is likely to grow and therefore some compromise has to be made between the need for instant or quick effect and long-term value. Most of the trees discussed on pp.152–176 should not grow too large for 20 to 25 years, but a few like *Cedrus deodara* will do so after 15 years. It is a personal decision whether you wish to enjoy such trees temporarily and commit yourself to felling them in about 20 years' time.

THE NATURE OF THE SITE

For further details of individual trees and their preference for or intolerance of certain conditions, see the descriptions on pp.152–176 and the table on pp.178–180.

Soil. Trees will adapt to a wide range of conditions and it is always possible to find suitable ones for difficult soils which are wet or waterlogged, over chalk or limestone, or dry and sandy. Only a few trees have positive dislikes. A good loam, containing a blend of clay, silt and sand particles with a sprinkling of organic matter, will ensure the best growth and the largest trees, but reasonable results can be obtained where there is a least 6 in. (15 cm) of top soil – that is, the upper soil layer, which is rich in nutrients, organic matter and earthworms.

The type of soil does, however, have a marked effect on the rate of establishment and growth. Thus many trees will grow satisfactorily on heavy clay soils which tend to be wet, but on very sticky clays they may take several seasons before starting to make significant new growth. Either this has to be accepted, or the process must be speeded up, by choosing a larger specimen in the first place or by improving the soil. Alternatively, the tree can be planted on a small mound for better drainage.

Both heavy clay and light sandy soils can be improved by adding organic matter in the form of well rotted compost or

Opposite: *Cedrus deodara*, the deodar, is much more attractive as a young tree, when it is dense and shapely with the hanging branch tips

Above: *Laurus nobilis*, the bay tree, a native of the Mediterranean region, thrives in coastal conditions, but may be damaged by frost

Below: Even at an early age, *Catalpa bignonioides* 'Aurea' has very large leaves and a naturally low and spreading habit

manure and, if necessary, by putting in drainage to carry water away from the site. Compacted soil is a common problem, especially on land surrounding newly built houses where earthmoving machinery has been used. In a small garden, the most practical method to overcome this and produce a loose open soil, which is beneficial to growth, is double digging. This involves digging to a depth of two spits or spade depths. The first spit (topsoil) is put aside, then the subsoil is dug over and covered with topsoil.

Climate. Despite considerable variation in climate over the length of Britain, many of the trees suitable for small gardens will thrive throughout the country. However, there are some, such as *Arbutus unedo* and *Laurus nobilis*, which are hardy only in the milder districts of southern and western Britain and may require winter protection or the shelter of a wall, particularly in the colder east and north. Unpredictable spring frosts are a general hazard of the British climate, often spoiling young buds or foliage.

Aspect. On the whole, trees prefer an open aspect with full sunlight to grow, flower and fruit well, but will tolerate some shade or being in shadow for part of the day. In dense shade, the choice is more limited, although hollies and cotoneaster, for instance, will flourish. Shade influences the growth of trees, usually making them taller, narrower and more open.

Exposure. Exposure to wind will slow the growth rate and harm the appearance of all trees. Damage is due partly to physical abrasion between twigs and leaves and partly to the drying effect of the wind. Some trees, like *Catalpa bignonioides*, have large floppy leaves which will not stand any battering by the wind, but others, including many pines, willows, rowans and whitebeams, will grow satisfactorily, if more slowly, in exposed situations.

On coasts, exposure tend to be more severe, with nothing to reduce the wind speed as it comes off the sea and salt spray adding to its harmful effects. Nevertheless, some trees, among them juniper and hawthorn, will succeed in these conditions. (See also the Wisley Handbook, *Seaside Gardening.*)

Purchasing and Planting

TYPES OF TREE

The trees offered by nurseries range from young transplants 1 to 2 ft (30–60 cm) tall, as used in forestry and motorway landscape planting, to semi-mature trees 30–35 ft (10 m) tall, which are appropriate for prestigious developments or instant effect. For owners of small gardens, the choice will probably be confined to trees between 20 in. and 13 ft (0.5–4 m) tall.

Most are sold as standard, half standard or feathered trees. All are from 6½ to 13 ft (2–4 m) tall, with a number of branches in the crown, and have been grown in the nursery for several years. A standard has had the branches removed from the lower 6 ft (1.8 m) of the stem to give a clean stem; in a half standard, the clean stem is shorter, around 3 to 5 ft (1–1.5 m). Both are useful when definite clearance above ground level is needed, or for displaying an attractive bark. On a feathered tree, the small side branches are retained in the nursery, which results in a tree with foliage to the ground. This can be better in natural planting.

Smaller trees, under 6½ ft (2 m), are cheaper to buy and, with proper care, will give as good a return in five years. Less common trees, those which are difficult to transplant and evergreens often have to be acquired at this size.

Trees are available as bare-rooted, root-balled or container-grown plants. Those sold as bare-rooted have been lifted from the ground in the nursery and all the soil shaken off. They should only be bought if the roots are wrapped in damp straw, or similar moisture-retentive material, bound in place by a sheet of poly-thene or hessian. This is appropriate for deciduous trees, which may be planted during the winter season while dormant.

Root-balled trees have been lifted with the nursery soil attached to the roots, which are usually wrapped in hessian. This can help to ensure the survival of large specimens, trees which are temperamental about transplanting, such as birches, and evergreens. However, it makes them awkward to move and they must be handled carefully to avoid damaging the root ball. They are also more expensive and not generally recommended for private gardens.

Container-grown trees are potted up into a container about a year before being put on sale. The advantages are that the tree should not suffer any check from loss of roots, as it does when lifted, and that it can be planted at any time of year, not just in the winter planting season. This explains why trees from garden centres are normally container-grown, since most of their sales occur in the months of April to June. Evergreens and trees with thick fleshy roots can also be more safely planted if container-grown. A tree which has spent less than three months in the pot should not be purchased, because the roots will not have grown into the compost and this will fall away during planting. A tree which has been in the same pot for two years or more should also be rejected, as it will probably be pot-bound. This happens when the roots become cramped and grow round the pot; once planted, they will continue to do so, rather than spreading out into the soil and forming a strong root system. Such trees rarely thrive and often collapse or are blown down after a few seasons.

Many trees, particularly selected forms which will not come true from seed, are in fact grafted on to a rootstock of the same or a related species.

WHEN AND WHERE TO BUY

Trees can be obtained from nurseries in person, or by mail order if they are reputable firms, from garden centres and from the plant sales outlets of gardens open to the public – often a good source of the unusual. Generally, bare-rooted trees should be purchased and planted only during the period November to early March. Container-grown trees may be bought at other times, although it is wise to avoid the midsummer months, July and August, when they will be growing vigorously and need frequent watering.

PLANTING

The first stage in planting a tree is to excavate a hole or pit. This should be dug at least 6 in. (15 cm) larger in each direction than the spread of the roots or the size of the container. The bottom of the pit should be forked over and the surfaces of the sides should also be broken if these are compacted or glazed, to allow the roots of the tree to spread and penetrate the surrounding soil without difficulty. Loose soil should then be placed back in the pit, so that it is as deep as the depth of the roots of the tree, but no more: trees are planted, not buried! Peat or compost can be added to this soil, making up about a quarter of the volume. Peat is particularly advisable for a container-grown tree, which will have been growing in a peat mixture, and it will help the roots adjust to the new conditions. If a stake if required, it should be driven in at this stage, in order not to damage the roots of the tree (see p.143).

When planting in a lawn, turf should be removed from the area of the pit and either used elsewhere or put in the bottom of the pit. It should not be placed on the surface of the soil around the tree, as the grass and weeds will grow, even upside down, and compete for moisture and nutrients to the detriment of the tree.

The roots of a bare-rooted tree should be unwrapped from their protective covering and spread out in the hole. Any that are badly damaged or broken can be cut out, but the root system should be reduced as little as possible. Work the soil between the roots and gently firm in each layer with the foot, taking care not to injure the roots or to stamp on them. Continue until the soil level is the same as that in the nursery, which will show as a dark mark on the bark.

The roots of a container-grown tree may be circling the bottom of the pot, in which case they should either be teased out or the outer spiral should be cut at three or four points, going no deeper into the compost than $\frac{1}{2}$ in. (1 cm), so that new spreading roots are formed. If the plant is pot-bound, with very woody circling roots, it should be returned to the supplier.

A root-balled tree should be placed in the pit before untying the hessian and cutting away at the sides. Any hessian beneath the root ball can be left to rot away.

If the weather prevents immediate planting, trees should be kept in a cool shed until conditions improve. Container-grown and properly packed bare-rooted trees will not suffer, so long as the roots do not dry out.

WATERING

All trees benefit from being watered immediately after planting. This often causes the soil to settle slightly and the next day, after the water has drained, it is sensible to firm the soil again around the tree. Even in the winter, newly planted trees should be watered during dry periods. Watering is especially important with evergreens, which continue to lose moisture from the leaves but may be unable to replace it from the surrounding soil until root growth starts in early spring. Spraying their foliage with water once or twice a day for a fortnight is also helpful, particularly for non-container-grown evergreens planted in late spring and early autumn. However, it is no substitute for keeping the soil moist but not waterlogged.

PROTECTION

Some form of temporary shelter will aid the establishment of trees when they are planted in full leaf with bare roots or poor root

Above left: *Chamaecyparis nootkatensis* 'Pendula', with distinctive long drooping branchlets
Above right: *Betula utilis*, the Himalayan birch, displays its bark to advantage when planted alone on a lawn
Below right: The large decorative fruits of *Malus × robusta* 'Red Siberian' persist well into winter
Below left: A newly planted tree with a stake to keep the roots firm and the soil built up in layers

balls, for example, evergreens during winter, or on very exposed sites. A hessian screen may be used, or a large polythene bag, which must be open at both top and bottom otherwise the heat generated by the sun will kill the tree. Similar protection can be given in subsequent winters to trees which are tender when young, such as *Arbutus* and *Eucryphia*.

STAKING

Small trees of less than $3\frac{1}{4}$ ft (1 m) should not require staking except on very windy sites. Trees 3 to 6 ft (1–2 m) tall may need some support and here a bamboo cane will suffice. The tree should be secured to the cane with plastic tape, which expands in hot weather and is pliable, not with wire or string, which cuts into the tree as it grows and does not rot or yield.

For larger trees of $6\frac{1}{2}$ ft (2 m) or more, staking may be necessary. The role of a stake is to hold the roots firm while the tree gets established. The traditional wisdom was to have the stake the same height as the tree, but although this prevents rocking, it is bad for the development of the stem. The stem serves two functions: a small part of it contains tissues which transport water and nutrients between the roots and the crown; most of it is devoted to keeping the top of the tree above the ground where it belongs. Any bending of the stem caused by the wind enables the tree to determine the amount of wood required for purposes of support. However, if a tree is held rigid by a solid stake, the stem does not bend and little structural wood is made. The stem may even be deformed and become greater in diameter above the top tie than it is nearer the ground, instead of being shaped in a desirable steady taper. The consequence is that when the stake is removed or breaks, the tree cannot sustain the crown and falls over.

A short stake about 3 ft (1 m) long will achieve the objective of securing the tree while the roots grow into the soil and will let the stem thicken naturally. Having dug the planting hole, the stake should be driven in near the centre, close to where the stem will be, and should extend approximately 12 to 20 in. (30–50 cm) above soil level. The tree is then planted and attached to it with a plastic tree tie placed at the top of the stake. If the stem itself needs support – and a thin-stemmed tree like *Malus* often does – a bamboo cane should be used in addition. The stake can usually be removed after the second winter, preferably in spring as the tree is about to come in to leaf, and the cane can be taken away at the same time (see figure, opposite).

Maintenance

ESTABLISHING A NEWLY PLANTED TREE

The main essential in establishing a newly planted tree, provided it has been properly planted, is to ensure that it does not die from want of moisture during the first couple of seasons. Water can, and should, be given during dry periods in the summer, when at least 4 gallons (15 l) should be applied to the soil immediately around the tree once a week. However, it is much more important to supply the plant with adequate moisture before the soil has dried out, not after. Control of competing weeds is the most effective way of doing this and also allows the tree alone to utilize the nutrients available in the soil, which increases early growth and in itself hastens establishment.

Weeds can be kept in check by traditional means such as hoeing and hand weeding, by using chemical herbicides such as glyphosate (available to amateurs as Tumbleweed), or by applying a mulch. This can be of bark, peat, leaf-mould or other organic matter, or of thick black polythene. The mulch is best put on in the spring, before the ground has become dry, in a layer about 2 in. (5 cm) deep, and will also help to conserve moisture. Whichever method is followed, an area of at least 11 sq. ft (1 m²) around the tree should be kept free of weeds and competing plants, especially grass and clover, for the first two years.

FEEDING

In most gardens, trees do not require fertilizing. However, growth may be enhanced by using either a mulch of well rotted compost or manure, or a chemical fertilizer. A general purpose fertilizer, with an analysis of around 7 to 10 parts each of nitrogen, phosphorus and potassium, is appropriate, at a rate of 2 oz per sq. yd (67 g per m²).

With a young tree it is especially important to apply fertilizer to clean earth, which is free from grass and weeds, otherwise they and not the tree will benefit and make the increased growth; the tree may even be set back as a result of greater competition. With a mature tree, fertilizer can be placed in holes drilled in the ground. It may also be scattered on the soil surface, weeds and all, and will probably work down to the roots within a year or so, provided any grass cuttings are left to rot and not collected.

PRUNING

In a small garden, pruning may be necessary at two stages – first to form a young tree of the desired habit and, second, to control the growth of a mature tree.

Formative pruning. Any weak or crossing branches must be removed, as they will die or rub together, permitting the entry of disease and decay. Certain trees naturally develop a single leader or main stem, which can be seen as a continuation of the trunk, but surplus leaders sometimes arise. These should be cut off when the tree is small, before its appearance is spoilt and it becomes weakened. Similarly, on trees where a clear stem or specified ground clearance is required, unwanted side branches should be removed, including low feathers, before they grow too large.

It is important to carry out formative pruning while the tree is still young and small: a cut only 1 in. (2–3 cm) in diameter will heal more quickly and leave less of a scar than one 4 in. (10 cm) in diameter. Branches should be cut off at the base, just outside the collar of growth.

With variegated trees, any shoots which revert and produce normal green foliage should be cut out below the point of reversion. Apart from destroying the effect of the tree, the green portion tends to grow faster than the variegated part and can quickly take over.

Pruning mature trees. Larger trees can be kept within bounds to some extent by pruning. This is never entirely satisfactory, but may be preferable to removing the tree and waiting for a replacement to grow. Most trees will make new growth if simply hacked but this is not recommended. It encourages disease, results in poorer production of flowers and fruit and leads to excessive regrowth, which often means that the tree is as large or as dense as before within three or four years and looks ugly in winter without the leaves.

Where it is necessary to prune a tree, the object should be to diminish the density or spread of the foliage as unobtrusively as possible. The first can be achieved by removing surplus branches which are cut off where they join the stem or the main branch Cuts should be made at a point just outside the collar formed around the base of the branch, in such a way as to prevent the weight of the branch tearing off a strip of bark (see figure, p.31). The spread can also be reduced, without destroying the overall shape, by shortening long branches. Where there is a side branch or fork in the branch, the larger portion is cut off, leaving the tree

Above: *Cornus controversa* 'Variegata', a small tree of elegant and unusual shape with the bonus of variegated foliage

Below: The great white cherry, *Prunus* 'Tai Haku', may grow up to 25 ft (7.5 m) high and more in width; it flowers in April

Opposite: Normally a large upright shrub, *Corylopsis veitchiana* produces fragrant primrose yellow blossom in April and has purplish young leaves

with a similar outline but a smaller spread. Current research shows that tree paints and wound dressings are of very little benefit and best avoided. Neatly sawn wounds will generally heal more quickly if left bare (see figure opposite).

Pruning may be carried out at any season on most trees, with a few exceptions. Cherries are best pruned in midsummer, as there is less risk of infection by silver-leaf disease and of the tree producing a lot of gum. Birches and maples should also be pruned in summer and may bleed badly if cut during the period from mid-winter until they are in full leaf. On the whole, if trees are being cut back hard, it is wiser to do this early in the year, when new growth will quickly follow, rather than in late summer, when any subsequent regrowth may not be hardy enough to withstand early autumn frosts. This applies especially to evergreen trees. With conifers, it is important not to cut back into dead brown foliage and to ensure that green leaves are present on the shoots below the cuts, in order for new growth to occur.

Root suckers sometimes appear on grafted trees and can be a problem, as they will often grow faster than the intended top. They should be severed with a spade where they arise from the underground root or stem. Suckers on the bole or lower trunk should be rubbed out in early summer while they are still soft.

Damage caused by the weather should be repaired. Branches broken by wet snow or storms should be cut back to sound side branches and any parts of branches or twigs harmed by cold or frost should be removed. Be cautious, however. The foliage of many evergreen trees can appear badly damaged and brown without the tree suffering any significant injury and it is always sensible to wait until summer to see if the tree is coming into leaf.

TRAINING SHRUBS AS TREES

The distinction between a tree and a shrub is not always clear cut. A number of taller-growing plants, which are commonly regarded as shrubs, can be trained to make a single stem and look like small trees. The process tends to be slower than with true trees, but a shrub treated in this way can be useful as a replacement for a tree which has outgrown its space.

The principle is to select a vigorous vertical shoot to form the main stem and to cut out any competing growths. The stem may need to be held upright with a cane and any shoots arising from the base should be removed, preferably at an early stage in their growth before they become woody.

Some suitable shrubs are mentioned on pp.152–176; see also the chapters on shrubs, beginning on p.182.

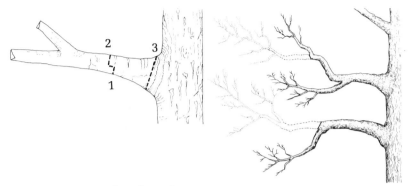

Above: How to cut a large branch – 1) first, make the undercut to stop the bark tearing; 2) next, cut above that to remove the branch; 3) finally, tidy up the stump

Above right: Top, cutting back to a fork; below, removing a surplus branch

'Red Cascade', a particularly free-fruiting cultivar of the native spindle tree *Euonymus europaeus*

PESTS AND DISEASES

Trees can be afflicted with a number of pests and diseases, but fortunately these are rarely a serious problem, more often simply a nuisance.

The chief pests are aphids, scale insects and caterpillars, which feed mainly on buds, leaves and shoots and can be troublesome or, on young trees, positively harmful. However, they may be dealt with by spraying a suitable insecticide, or on deciduous plants by applying a tar oil winter wash when growth is fully dormant. Such measures should also help prevent the development of sooty mould, which is caused by sap-feeding insects, while mildews and other diseases may often be controlled by using a fungicide. Two of the most devastating diseases are honey fungus and fireblight and, if symptoms of these are suspected, it is wise to seek expert advice. Otherwise, good general hygiene in the garden, correct planting and aftercare and careful pruning should help to keep trees healthy and reasonably free from pests and diseases.

Young trees can be damaged by rabbits gnawing the bark or by cats sharpening their claws on the trunk. Protection can be given with a proprietary tree guard, or one made out of chicken wire or polythene netting. Whatever material is used, it should not constrict or cut into the stem of the tree.

An excellent reference book on this subject, which the reader should consult for further information, is *Garden Pests and Diseases*, by Audrey Brooks and Andrew Halstead.

A Selection of Trees for Small Gardens

This chapter describes some of the many different trees which are suitable for small gardens. The criteria for the selection are that the tree is attractive as a small specimen 13 to 33 ft (4–10 m) tall and that it is reasonably easy to obtain. Most of the trees discussed are widely available from garden centres, as well as from the larger mail order suppliers. However, a few may need searching for in specialist nurseries or plant sales outlets attached to gardens open to the public. I hope that mentioning these less common ones will encourage gardeners to plant a greater range of trees, rather than relying on just a few which, while excellent in themselves, can be tiresome when over-used.

It must be emphasized that the height of a tree depends both on its inherent character and on the conditions of the site where it is growing. Trees will grow taller on good soils than they will on poor soils. They also tend to be lower and more spreading when grown in full sunlight or an exposed position, but taller and narrower when in heavy shade. All these factors, together with the size of the tree at the time of planting, should be borne in mind when referring to the likely heights indicated in the descriptions below.

The trees are treated in alphabetical order of genus, although within each genus species and forms are often grouped according to similarities. If the tree is evergreen or semi-evergreen, this fact is noted, otherwise it is deciduous.

A descriptive word for the habit – i.e. fastigiate (or narrowly columnar), upright, conical, spreading, domed, weeping – is given at the end of the entry, followed by two sets of figures, showing the estimated height and the diameter of the crown after 10 years and after 20 to 25 years respectively. Types of soil are mentioned only when a tree is intolerant of a particular soil or when it is especially useful on a difficult soil.

Further guidance on choosing trees for specific purposes or situations will be found in the table on pp.178–180, which summarizes the requirements and features of the trees discussed in this chapter. Satisfactory small trees can also be made from a number of the taller-growing shrubs (see p.148).

Abies The silver firs make narrow, crowned, upright, evergreen trees with rather spaced or whorled branching and are usually available as small plants less than 3¼ ft (1 m) tall. They are not long-lived on dry or chalky soils.

A. *koreana* (Korean fir) has blue-green cones, which are freely carried on small trees, and short leaves of vivid silver on the undersides. Conical; 6½ x 5 ft (2 x 1.5 m); 16 x 10 ft (5 x 3 m).

A. *forrestii* has much larger cones of a brighter violet-blue, but these are not produced on such young trees. The leaves are longer and also bright silver beneath, set on reddish shoots. Conical; 13 x 6½ ft (4 x 2 m); 33 x 13 ft (10 x 4 m).

A. *concolor* (Colorado fir) is useful for its fine blue or grey foliage and will thrive on drier sites than the other two, although it will probably grow too large after 15 years. Conical; 23 x 10 ft (7 x 3 m); 46 x 16 ft (14 x 5 m).

Acer Maples are not generally noticeable for the flowers, but most display good autumn foliage and several have decorative barks.

A. *capillipes* is one of the snakebark maples, so called because of the white or pale stripes which snake up the otherwise green bark. The winter shoots are bright red and the slightly lobed, glossy leaves turn orange and scarlet in autumn. Spreading; 20 x 13 ft (6 x 4 m); 33 x 20 ft (10 x 6 m).

Three related species of similar habit are: A. *davidii*, with the bark having brighter white markings, although less reliable autumn colour; A. *grosseri* var. *hersii*, with a beautiful bark and foliage turning red or yellow; and A. *pensylvanicum* (moosewood), with a handsome bark and large leaves becoming yellow in autumn.

A. *cappadocicum* (Caucasian maple): 'Aureum' has leaves of pale bright yellow when they emerge, slowly changing to green after a few weeks and assuming a brilliant gold in autumn. Domed; 10 x 6½ ft (3 x 2 m); 20 x 13 ft (6 x 4 m).

A. *griseum* (paperbark maple) has fiery red autumn colour and a bark of bright red-brown, which is shed in small paper-thin sheets and gives an attractive shaggy appearance, especially in winter. Upright dome; 10 x 6½ ft (3 x 2 m); 16 x 10 ft (5 x 3 m).

A. *japonicum* (fullmoon maple) develops brilliant scarlets, golds and purples in autumn. Upright; 10 x 5 ft (3 x 1.5 m); 20 x 10 ft (6 x 3 m).

A. *negundo* (box elder): 'Variegatum' has leaves irregularly margined with a broad white zone, giving a marbled effect, but it is inclined to revert to pure green. Spreading; 26 x 16 ft (8 x 5 m); 36 x 26 ft (11 x 8 m). (See p.130.)

A. *palmatum* (Japanese maple) is normally grown in the form of one its numerous cultivars, most often sold as small plants around 3¼–5 ft (1–1.5 m) tall. They can be damaged by winter cold in exposed situations and are not suitable for shallow chalk soils. Domed; 10 x 6½ ft (3 x 2 m); 20 x 16 ft (6 x 5 m). 'Atropurpureum' has bright purple new foliage which is somewhat overwhelming in midsummer but turns crimson-purple in autumn. 'Osakazuki' has green leaves which in autumn adopt a series of attractive hues over several weeks, finally turning a brilliant flame-scarlet. 'Senkaki' has smaller leaves becoming yellow in autumn and the one-year-old shoots are coral-red in winter. (See p.130.)

A. *pseudoplatanus* (sycamore): 'Brilliantissimum' has new leaves which emerge shrimp-pink, changing through yellow or orange to a marbled green. 'Prince Handjery' is similar, with the leaves tinged purple beneath. Domed; 6½ x 3¼ ft (2 x 1 m); 10 x 6½ ft (3 x 2 m).

Aesculus Horse chestnut

A. *neglecta* 'Erythroblastos' has new leaves of bright pink, turning to yellow and then green. The young foliage can be damaged by spring frosts. Upright; 10 x 6½ ft (3 x 2 m); 16 x 10 ft (5 x 3 m).

Alnus Alder

A. *incana* (grey alder): 'Aurea' has softly yellow leaves and yellow shoots which

Above: *Abies koreana*, like most of the silver firs, prefers a rich moist soil but is tolerant of shade

Below: *Acer japonicum* does best in a moist well drained position away from cold winds

become orange over winter. The male catkins are a rich red, changing to orange-red when expanded in early spring. Upright; 16 × 6½ ft (5 × 2 m); 26 × 13 ft (8 × 4 m). 'Pendula' is similar but weeping; 16 × 13 ft (5 × 4 m); 20 × 20 ft (6 × 6 m). Both forms will grow equally well on wet and dry soils, less so on chalky ones.

Aralia
A. elata (devil's walking stick, Japanese angelica tree) carries enormous compound leaves and bears large clusters of white flowers in September. It is not suitable for gardens frequented by young children, as the stems and leaves are covered with small stout spines. Suckers appear from the base which should be removed to prevent it becoming too shrubby. Domed; 16 × 10 ft (5 × 3 m); 26 × 16 ft (8 × 5 m).

Arbutus
A. unedo (strawberry tree) has small dark leaves and bears ivory-white flowers in small clusters in October and November. The strawberry-like fruits ripen the following autumn and are edible but unpalatable. It is evergreen and young plants need winter protection in exposed gardens. Domed; 10 × 6½ ft (3 × 2 m); 16 × 10 ft (5 × 2 m).

Betula Birches are planted for the attractive bark, the delicate and often light foliage, the male catkins with the leaves in spring and the autumn colour. They must have an open situation, as they do not tolerate shade. They have aggressive surface roots and few plants can be grown satisfactorily beneath them.
B. medwediewii has light yellow leaves in autumn, with glossy brown shoots and large buds in winter. Domed; 8 × 6½ ft (2.5 × 2 m); 16 × 16 ft (5 × 5 m).
B. nigra (river birch) has a shaggy, pinkish orange bark and will tolerate wet soils. Upright; 13 × 6½ ft (4 × 2 m); 26 × 13 ft (8 × 4 m).
B. pendula (silver birch): 'Dalecarlica' has drooping branches and deeply cut leaves. Upright; 26 × 10 ft (8 × 3 m); 49 × 16 ft (15 × 5 m). 'Youngii' makes a cascading mound, usually not growing taller than the height of the stem on to which it was grafted in the nursery. Weeping; 10 × 10 ft (3 × 3 m); 13 × 20 ft (4 × 6 m).
B. utilis (Himalayan birch) has a bark which ranges in colour from mahogany to dazzling white. The trees with very white barks are usually listed as B. jacquemontii. Upright; 20 × 6½ ft (6 × 2 m); 39 × 16 ft (12 × 5 m). (See p.142.) 'Sauwala White' is smaller, with a very white bark; 13 × 6½ ft (4 × 2 m); 26 × 23 ft (8 × 4 m).

Calocedrus
C. decurrens (incense cedar) is an evergreen conifer of distinctive columnar shape, with fans of bright green foliage. Unlike the related cypresses, it is resistant to honey fungus. Fastigiate; 16 × 3¼ ft (5 × 1 m); 36 × 6½ ft (11 × 2 m). (See p.155.)

Carpinus Hornbeam
C. turczaninowii has small densely borne leaves which turn russet in autumn and it thrives on heavy clay soils. Upright; 10 × 6½ ft (3 × 2 m); 20 × 13 ft (6 × 4 m).

Catalpa
C. bignonioides (Indian bean tree) produces large panicles of spotted white flowers in July and the heart-shaped leaves are up to 10 in. (24 cm) across. Spreading; 20 × 10 ft (6 × 3 m); 30 × 20 ft (9 × 6 m). 'Aurea' has bright yellow foliage, fading towards the end of summer and when grown in shade, but does not flower; 13 × 10 ft (4 × 3 m); 20 × 13 ft (6 × 4 m). Neither can withstand exposure and they are only suitable for sheltered locations in the southern half of Britain. (See p.137.)

Cedrus Cedar
C. deodara (deodar) has bluish green foliage and short horizontal branches which are emphatically pendulous at the tips. An evergreen, it will eventually grow too tall, but is very attractive for 15 to 20 years. Upright weeping; 26 × 6½ ft (8 × 2 m); 39 × 13 ft (12 × 4 m). (See p.136.)

Cercidiphyllum
C. japonicum (Katsura tree) has delicate, small, heart-shaped leaves which are bright pink when young and assume a rich variety of autumn tints in favourable

154

seasons. The new leaves may be damaged by spring frosts, but the tree will produce fresh ones. Upright; 23 × 10 ft (7 × 3 m); 39 × 20 ft (12 × 6 m). (See p.181.)

Cercis

C. siliquastrum (Judas tree) carries abundant clusters of purple flowers in May, emerging from buds on old wood and often from the trunk itself. It is adapted to hot dry locations and will thrive on chalk or limestone. Domed; 10 × 6½ ft (3 × 2 m); 16 × 10 ft (5 × 3 m). (See p.157.)

C. canudensis (redbud): 'Forest Pansy', of similar shape and size, has striking purple foliage from spring into August and gives bright reddish purple colours in autumn, but is not free-flowering.

Chamaecyparis Cypresses are the most commonly planted evergreen conifers and range from tall trees of 66 ft (20 m) or more to dwarf trees suitable for rock gardens. They are not tolerant of waterlogged soils.

C. lawsoniana (Lawson cypress) produces interesting variations in foliage colour and habit when raised from seed and these make good evergreen screens without growing too tall too fast. Fastigiate or upright; 13 × 3¼ ft (4 × 1 m); 33–49 × 10–16 ft (10–15 × 3–5 m). Named forms, which are usually planted as specimen trees, also provide a range of different shapes and tree colours. They include 'Allumii', spire-like with bluish foliage; 'Columnaris', with paler grey-blue foliage and columnar habit; 'Kilmacurragh', very narrowly fastigiate with bright green leaves; 'Lane' and 'Stewartii', with golden yellow foliage sprays; and 'Pembury Blue', with bright blue-grey leaves in pendulous sprays on a broadly conical tree.

C. nootkatensis 'Pendula' has an open crown of level branches with foliage hanging vertically in flat sprays. Conical weeping. (See p.142.)

C. obtusa (Hinoki cypress): 'Crippsii' has bright gold foliage. Conical; both 8 × 3 ft (2.5 × 1 m); 20 × 10 ft (6 × 3 m).

Cornus The dogwoods are a large genus which includes several small trees.

C. controversa (table dogwood) has remarkable level tiers of foliage on horizontal branches and large clusters of creamy white flowers carried above these in June. 'Variegata' is an exquisite slower-growing form, with the leaves margined creamy white. Upright conical; 16 × 6½ ft (5 × 2m); 23 × 10 ft (7 × 3 m). (See p.146.)

C. kousa var. *chinensis* has flowers surrounded by four large creamy white bracts and borne above the foliage in June on horizontal branches. These are followed by edible strawberry-like fruits and attractive red-tinted dying leaves in autumn. Upright conical; 10 × 6½ ft (3 × 2 m); 20 × 10 ft (6 × 3 m). (See p.159.)

Corylus Hazel

C. avellana, the native hazel, is often grown for its edible nuts. It has fresh yellow catkins hanging from the branches in late winter and the leaves turn russet in autumn. It tends to be shrubby, with many stems and suckers arising from the base, but is useful for screening. Domed; 13 × 13 ft (4 × 4 m); 20 × 20 ft (6 × 6 m).

Cotoneaster

C. 'Cornubia' is semi-evergreen and has small, white, hawthorn-scented flowers in summer, its chief glory being the profusion of large red berries in autumn. Spreading; 16 × 10 ft (5 × 3 m); 26 × 20 ft (8 × 6 m). *C. frigidus* is very similar, with larger leaves. Both need pruning and training to one stem when young to develop as trees (see p.148).

C. glaucophyllus is more of a spreading shrub and more fully evergreen. The leaves are greyish blue beneath and the small fruits are orange-red, colouring late, around Christmas, to give a welcome bonus of colour at that season.

Previous page: With its narrow habit, *Calocedrus decurrens* is ideal planted as a single specimen or in a group and deserves to be more widely grown

Crataegus Hawthorn

C. monogyna (common hawthorn, may) is initially upright and becomes more spreading, with pendulous tips to the branches. It is wreathed with fragrant white flowers in May, followed by the purplish red haws or fruits; 13 × 6½ ft (4 × 2 m); 23 × 16 ft (7 × 5 m). *C. oxycantha* 'Paul's Scarlet' has double scarlet flowers. *C. prunifolia* has glossy leaves which change to rich crimson in autumn. The large red fruits remain on the tree after the leaves are lost.

Cupressus Cypress

C. glabra (smooth cypress) has a smooth reddish or deep purple bark. The yellow male catkins contrast with the evergreen blue foliage in autumn. It is especially suitable for hot, dry or chalky soils. Conical; 16 × 6½ ft (5 × 2 m); 33 × 13 ft (10 × 4 m).

Decaisnea

D. fargesii has stout shoots covered in a waxy bloom and large pinnate leaves (made up of leaflets) nearly 3 ft (90 cm) long. Yellowish green flowers in May are followed by the large, waxy, metallic blue pods in autumn. It is not recommended for sites where spring frosts are common. Upright; 10 × 6½ ft (3 × 2 m); 16 × 13 ft (5 × 4 m).

Embothrium

E. coccineum (fire bush) is a flamboyant tree in May and June when covered in the brilliant crimson-scarlet or orange-scarlet tubular flowers. It is evergreen and will tolerate some shade, but must have a moist acidic soil and a sheltered site. Fastigiate; 20 × 3¼ ft (6 × 1 m); 30 × 5 ft (9 × 1.5 m).

Eucalyptus

E. gunnii (cider gum), a hardy evergreen, will become too large within 10 years if left to grow naturally. It can be cut back to ground level or a short stem annually in spring and will make new growths with bright blue foliage of up to 10 ft (3 m) in a season. Upright; 33 × 10 ft (10 × 3 m); 66 × 26 ft (20 × 8 m). (See p.161.)

E. niphophila (snow gum) is another hardy species, evergreen and slower-growing. It has mahogany-coloured new leaves turning glossy green, twigs which are shiny dark red in winter, becoming covered with a waxy bloom in spring, and a creamy white bark. Domed; 16 × 10 ft (5 × 3 m); 26 × 20 ft (8 × 6 m).

Eucryphia

E. × nymansensis 'Nymansay' has dark green, evergreen leaves showing off the large white flowers, which are profusely borne in August and early September once the tree is a few years old. It will grow on all soils, including chalky ones, but can be tender when young and is not suited to cold northern gardens. Upright; 16 × 3¼ ft (5 × 1 m); 30 × 10 ft (9 × 3 m).

Euonymus Spindle tree

E. europaeus 'Red Cascade' has rosy red fruits on weeping branches, giving a fine autumn effect. Upright; 10 × 3¼ ft (3 × 1 m); 16 × 10 ft (5 × 3 m). (See p.149.)

Fagus Beech

F. sylvatica 'Dawyck' has green foliage, while 'Dawyck Purple' has purple foliage and is slower-growing. Both make effective 'exclamation marks'. Fastigiate; 26 × 3¼ ft (8 × 1 m); 39 × 10 ft (12 × 3 m). 'Purpurea Pendula' grows only as tall as the stem on which it is trained or grafted, forming a complete cascade of purple leaves. Weeping; 10 × 6½ ft (3 × 2 m); 10 × 10 ft (3 × 3 m).

F. engleriana has sea-green foliage and, like other beeches, it will grow on acidic and alkaline sites, but does not tolerate heavy waterlogged soils. Domed; 13 × 6½ ft (4 × 2 m); 23 × 13 ft (7 × 4 m).

Previous page: As well as the magnificent flowers, *Cercis siliquastrum* has pretty heart-shaped leaves and, in winter, conspicuous long seed pods; it needs full sun and performs best in southern England

Above: *Cornus kousa* var. *chinensis*, blooming profusely at a time when many trees and shrubs are not in flower, benefits from a sunny position

Below: *Embothrium coccineum*, the spectacular fire bush, was originally introduced from Chile in 1846

Fraxinus Ash

F. mariesii bears creamy white flowers in June, followed in July by deep purple fruits. It will grow on a wide range of soils and deserves to be better known. Domed; 6½ × 3¼ ft (2 × 1 m); 13 × 10 ft (4 × 3 m).

F. velutina (Arizona ash) has velvety hairy shoots and leaves, the latter turning yellow in autumn. It is better suited to eastern England or a dry sunny site. Domed; 16 × 3¼–6½ ft (5 × 1–2 m); 23 × 6½–10 ft (7 × 2–3 m). (See p.162.)

Genista Broom

G. aetnensis (Mount Etna broom) has slender, almost leafless, green, rather pendulous shoots and is covered with fragrant, yellow, pea-like flowers in July and early August. The green branches give it the appearance of an evergreen. Upright; 16 × 3¼–6½ ft (5 × 1–2 m); 23 × 6½–10 ft (7 × 2–3 m). (See p.44.)

Ginkgo

G. biloba (maidenhair tree) has oily green, fan-shaped, curiously lobed leaves, which assume a beautiful golden yellow colour in late autumn. It will eventually grow too large for most gardens – the tree at Kew, planted in 1762, is now over 70 ft (21 m) tall – but as a young tree and for the first half century, it has a very narrow crown with little side branching. Fastigiate; 16 × 3¼ ft (5 × 1 m); 30 × 3¼–6½ ft (9 × 1–2 m).

Gleditsia

G. triacanthos (honey locust): 'Sunburst' has feathery pinnate or doubly pinnate foliage (composed of leaflets on each side of the stalk) which is golden yellow in spring and remains a fresh light or yellow green throughout the summer. It makes a very striking tree, better in full sun, although tolerating light shade. Domed; 16 × 6½ ft (5 × 2 m); 26 × 13 ft (8 × 4 m).

Halesia

H. monticola (mountain snowdrop tree) bears pendent, white, bell-shaped flowers in May, followed by curiously winged green fruits. Upright; 16 × 6½ ft (5 × 2 m); 26 × 13 ft (8 × 4 m). (See p.163.)

Hydrangea

H. paniculata is usually cultivated as a shrub, but can easily be trained into a small tree (see p.148). According to the form grown, conical white panicles of flowers are displayed from July ('Praecox'), through August and September ('Grandiflora'), to September and October ('Tardiva'). Spreading; 16 × 10 ft (5 × 3 m).

Ilex Hollies are useful for their evergreen foliage and long-persisting berries. Plants are normally either male or female and therefore both must be planted to ensure that the female produces berries. Hollies will grow well in shady locations, but can be difficult to move and are usually only available as small plants. Upright; 10 × 3¼ ft (3 × 1 m); 23 × 6½ ft (7 × 2 m).

I. aquifolium (common holly) has given rise to many attractive forms, including 'Amber', with numerous orange berries; 'Argentea Pendula', with grey-green leaves having a broad creamy white margin, many red berries and purplish pendulous shoots, which makes a small weeping tree; 'Golden Milkboy', male, with spiny leaves with a yellow centre; 'Handsworth New Silver', female, with leaves edged with cream and the similar 'Silver Queen', male (see p.163); and 'J. C. van Tol', one of the few hermaphrodite plants, which produces prolific red berries when planted on its own.

Eucalyptus gunni, the cider gum, has been recorded as reaching over 100 feet (30 m) high, although more often seen as a bushy medium-sized tree

Opposite: *Genista aetnensis* requires no more than a sunny spot and a well-drained soil to succeed and is completely hardy

Above: *Halesia monticola*, the mountain snowdrop tree, grows rapidly and flowers from an early age

Below: The boldly variegated 'Silver Queen', like other forms of *Ilex aquifolium*, adapts to almost any situation and soil

I. × *altaclarensis* (Highclere holly): 'Belgica Aurea' has leaves mottled grey-green with a yellow margin and 'Golden King' has red berries and green leaves splashed with grey and edged with gold.

Juniperus Junipers are usually obtainable as plants less than 3¼ ft (1 m) and are not likely to exceed a height of 10 ft (3 m) in 10 years. They are evergreen and especially recommended for hot, dry or chalky sites.

J. chinensis (Chinese juniper) is known in innumerable forms. 'Aurea' (Young's golden juniper) has golden foliage, becoming more pronounced on older plants, and massed yellow cones in April. 'Kaizuka' is a characterful plant, an erratically sprawling bush or small tree with bright green, dense foliage, often loaded with small greyish green berries or cones in autumn. Upright; 10 × 3¼ ft (3 × 1 m).

J. recurva (Himalayan juniper) has gracefully drooping branchlets, a flaky orange-brown bark and grey-green foliage. The variety *coxii* (coffin juniper) has longer needles of a mid-green colour. Weeping; 10 × 6½ ft (3 × 2 m); 16 × 10 ft (5 × 3 m).

J. scopulorum 'Skyrocket' is a distinctive pencil-thin tree with blue-grey foliage, the narrow crown usually being one tenth as wide as the plant is tall. It is useful as a punctuation mark in a scheme, or for creating a mini-avenue between two areas. Fastigiate; 13 × 1¼ ft (4 × 0.4 m); 26 × 1½ ft (8 × 0.5 m).

Koelreuteria

K. paniculata (pride of India) has large pinnate leaves consisting of oval leaflets, which turn yellow in autumn. In July and August it is covered in large panicles of numerous small yellow flowers, followed by unusual bladder-like fruits. For best development, it needs a warm sunny position in the southern and eastern parts of the country. Domed; 16 × 10 ft (5 × 3 m); 30 × 20 ft (9 × 6 m).

Laburnum

L. × *watereri* 'Vossii' bears large hanging racemes of yellow flowers up to 2 ft (60 cm) long in May and early June. It will not tolerate waterlogged soils. Spreading; 23 × 13 ft (7 × 4 m); 26 × 20 ft (8 × 6 m).

Laurus

L. nobilis (bay laurel) is evergreen and has leathery, dark green, aromatic leaves – the bayleaves used in cooking. Insignificant yellow flowers appear in late April and small black berries in the autumn. It is not fully hardy in central and northern districts, where it is susceptible to damage in severe winters and may be no more than a shrub. However, it will tolerate maritime exposure, and along the south coast grows taller than shown. It can be clipped into shape. Upright; 13 × 6½ ft (4 × 2 m); 26 × 16 ft (8 × 5 m). (See p.137.)

Ligustrum Privet

L. lucidum (Chinese privet) has glossy evergreen leaves and is valuable for the white flowers borne in large panicles in late August and September. It is quite unlike the generally perceived idea of a privet. 'Excelsum Superbum' is a form in which the leaves are margined and mottled with deep yellow and cream. In 'Tricolor', they have an irregular white border and are pinkish when young. Both are very striking small trees. Conical becoming domed; 13 × 6½ ft (4 × 2 m); 26 × 20 ft (8 × 6 m).

L. compactum has semi-evergreen lance-shaped leaves up to 6 in. (15 cm) long and is attractive in July when laden with white flowers. Domed; 13 × 6½ ft (4 × 2 m); 26 × 16 ft (8 × 5 m). *L. chenaultii* is similar, but with leaves to 10 in. (25 cm) long.

Lindera

L. obtusiloba produces yellow flowers in dense clusters on the twigs in March and April. The leaves may be entire or lobed, always prominently three-veined, and turn a fine butter-yellow in autumn. It is an unusual small tree, well worth considering if you want something out of the ordinary. Domed; 13 × 6½ ft (4 × 2 m); 23 × 13 ft (7 × 4 m).

Magnolia The magnolias have magnificent large flowers with fleshy petal and sepals (collectively called tepals), in some cases emerging before the leaves in spring, when they are susceptible to damage by frosts. The roots are thick and very fleshy, easily rotting if injured, and resent any disturbance or digging around them. Magnolias are best planted in early autumn or late April to May, when the roots are actively growing, and the ones mentioned here grow on most soils, including deep chalky soils. Apart from the flowers, the fruits are often ornamental, especially when opening to reveal the scarlet seeds.

M. delavayi is evergreen and has large, dull greyish green leaves up to 14 in. (35 cm) long. The creamy white, fragrant flowers, up to 8 in. (20 cm) across, are borne at the ends of the shoots. They last only a day but are carried in succession from late summer into autumn. Unfortunately, it is hardy only in the milder parts of the country; elsewhere it will be harmed in bad winters and should be grown against the wall of a house for shelter. Domed; 13 × 6½ ft (4 × 2 m); 23 × 13 ft (7 × 4 m).

M. grandiflora (bull bay, evergreen magnolia) has large, glossy, yellow-green leaves with rusty hairs beneath. The creamy white flowers, up to 10 in. (25 cm) across, have a spicy scent and are produced in successive flushes from July until the frosts in November. It is evergreen and hardy as a free-standing tree without wall protection in southern and western parts. Domed; 13 × 6½ ft (4 × 2 m); 23 × 13 ft (7 × 4 m).

M. kobus has pure white flowers up to 4 in. (10 cm) across. Although slow to bloom when young, after about 12 to 15 years a mature tree may be covered with literally hundreds of flowers in April. Domed; 13 × 6½ ft (4 × 2 m); 23 × 10 ft (7 × 3 m). Two hybrids, M. × loebneri 'Leonard Messel' and 'Merrill', make similar small trees but have the virtue of flowering from a young age. (See p.130.)

M. salicifolia (willow magnolia) carries the pure white flowers in late April on bare branches. These are less vulnerable to frost damage than those of other early-flowering magnolias and the tree blooms at a young age. Upright; 13 × 5 ft (4 × 1.5 m); 23 × 8 ft (7 × 2.5 m).

M. virginiana (sweet bay) is evergreen or deciduous and produces a constant succession of very fragrant, rather small, creamy white, later darkening, flowers from June until September. It is a choice but uncommon tree. Upright or domed; 13 × 5 ft (4 × 1.5 m); 20 × 10 ft (6 × 3 m).

M. wilsonii bears scented, white, cup-shaped, hanging flowers in May and June, best seen from below, and gives a further display in September with fruits and seeds. Spreading; 13 × 10 ft (4 × 3 m); 20 × 16 ft (6 × 5 m). M. sieboldii is similar, with flowers facing outwards. (See p.166.)

Mahonia

M. 'Charity' has bold, evergreen, prickly leaves and fragrant yellow flowers from October onwards. Although usually planted as a shrub, it grows into a tree with a distinctive ridged bark. Domed; 10 × 6½ ft (3 × 2 m); 23 × 13 ft (7 × 4 m).

Malus Crab

M. baccata (Siberian crab) is covered with massed white flowers in April, followed by small bright red or yellow crab-apples, which persist over winter. Spreading dome; 13 × 10 ft (4 × 3 m); 30 × 26 ft (9 × 8 m).

M. floribunda (Japanese crab) is bedecked in late April with flowers which are rosy red in bud, opening pale pink, and in autumn with red or yellow berries. Spreading; 10 × 6½ ft (3 × 2 m); 16 × 16 ft (5 × 5 m).

M. 'John Downie' has flowers pink in bud, opening white, and then conical yellow crab-apples 1 in. (3 cm) long, which may be used to make jelly. Upright becoming domed; 16 × 10 ft (5 × 3 m); 26 × 20 ft (8 × 6 m).

M. × robusta has white or pinkish flowers, followed by large fruits, red in 'Red Siberian' and yellow in 'Yellow Siberian', which remain into winter. Domed; 13 × 10 ft (4 × 3 m); 20 × 13 ft (6 × 4 m). (See p.142 and p.166.)

M. transitoria bears masses of small white flowers in late May and tiny yellow fruits which last long into winter. Spreading; 13 × 13 ft (4 × 4 m); 16 × 23 ft (5 × 7 m).

M. tschonoskii (Chonusuki crab) is a useful tree for confined spaces. The foliage

Above: The exotic large blooms of *Magnolia sieboldii* are followed by scarlet fruits and seeds

Below: The flowering crabs, including the familiar *Malus × robusta* 'Yellow Siberian', are undemanding small trees and flourish in all types of soil

Opposite: *Metasequoia glyptostroboides*, the only living representative of a prehistoric genus, was discovered in China in 1947

emerges silvery grey and turns a brilliant mixture of colours in the autumn. Conical; 23 × 10 ft (7 × 3 m); 36 × 20 ft (11 × 6 m).

Metasequoia
M. glyptostroboides (dawn redwood) thrives on both wet and dry soils. On the former it will grow too large after 15 years, but on the latter it slows down appreciably once it has reached 26–33 ft (8–10 m). It has fresh green foliage, becoming red in October and November, and fibrous orange-brown bark. Conical; 26 × 10 ft (8 × 3 m); 39 × 16 ft (12 × 5 m). (See p.167.)

Morus Mulberry
M. nigra (black mulberry) has large heart-shaped leaves and fruits changing from orange-scarlet to blackish purple in midsummer. Ripe mulberries are very tasty, but stain the fingers purple. Domed; 10 × 6½ ft (3 × 2 m); 16 × 16 ft (5 × 5 m).

Nothofagus Southern beech
N. antarctica (Antarctic beech) is a fast-growing tree similar in many respects to beech or birch, with small, usually balsam-scented leaves. It will not grow on chalk soils. Upright; 23 × 10 ft (7 × 3 m); 33 × 16 ft (10 × 5 m).

Nyssa
N. sylvatica (tupelo, black gum) has glossy leaves, which become bright red and yellow in autumn, and downturned branches. It will flourish on moist and acidic soils, but is not suitable for those over chalk. Conical; 13 × 6½ ft (4 × 2 m); 26 × 13 ft (8 × 4 m).

Picea Spruces are evergreen and are normally available as small trees less than 3 ft (1 m) tall. Any which grows too large can always be felled and the top used as a Christmas tree.
P. breweriana has horizontal side branches curtained with very long pendulous branchlets up to 6½ ft (2 m) in length. Plants which have been grafted should be purchased, as seedling trees take many years to develop this mature foliage. Upright; 10 × 6½ ft (3 × 2 m); 20 × 10 ft (6 × 3 m).
P. omorika (Serbian spruce) has a very narrow crown which, even when the tree ultimately reaches 50 ft (15 m) tall, is only 13 ft (4 m) wide and unlikely to become too spreading. It will grow at the same steady rate on wet, dry, acid or chalk soils. Conical; 16 × 3 ft (5 × 1 m); 26 × 5 ft (8 × 1.5 m).
P. orientalis (oriental spruce): 'Aurea' has very short needles, which are golden yellow for six weeks around June, afterwards turning dark green. The cones are brick-red and very attractive in April. Conical; 16 × 10 ft (5 × 3 m); 26 × 13 ft (8 × 4 m).
P. pungens (Colorado spruce, blue spruce) is invariably grown as one of its many forms, for instance, 'Glauca', 'Koster', 'Hoopsii' and 'Spekii', which have bright blue foliage and silvery blue new growth. A grafted plant may be slow to form an erect leader and the tree should be fed and watered to get it growing vigorously. Aphids cause the loss of needles and can be controlled by spraying with malathion or pirimicarb insecticides, either when the problem is noticed or as a precaution in late August. Conical; 10 × 6½ ft (3 × 2 m); 20 × 13 ft (6 × 4 m).

Pinus Pines have relatively long, evergreen leaves or needles, grouped in bundles of from two to five. They are especially suited to dry sandy sites.
P. aristata (bristlecone pine) has dark green needles flecked with white resin and bunched in fives. These are retained for up to 15 years and result in a densely crowned tree. Domed; 8 × 6½ ft (2.5 × 2 m); 16 × 13 ft (5 × 4 m).
P. bungeana (lacebark pine) has a grey-green bark, which peels off in small plates to reveal a creamy or pale yellow colour, gradually darkening to green, olive-brown, red or purple. It has leaves in threes. Conical; 10 × 6½ ft (3 × 2 m); 16 × 10 ft (5 × 3 m).
P. leucodermis (Bosnian pine) has dense, dark green needles in pairs and cones of a rich cobalt-blue in the summer of the second year, ripening to light brown. It is suitable for most soils, including those over chalk. Conical; 13 × 10 ft (4 × 3 m); 26 × 16 ft (8 × 5 m).

P. sylvestris (Scots pine): 'Aurea' has paired leaves which turn bright gold from December until April, the colour being particularly pronounced in cold weather, and for the rest of the year are bluish green. The male cones can be a good lemon-yellow in June. Conical; 13 × 10 ft (4 × 3 m); 26 × 13 ft (8 × 4 m).

Prunus Cherries will grow on a wide range of soils, but are not usually long-lived, especially on sandy or chalky soils. They are easy to transplant and quickly make effective trees.

P. 'Kursar' has vivid pink flowers in March and leaves colouring orange in autumn. Upright; 13 × 6½ ft (4 × 2 m); 20 × 10 ft (6 × 3 m). April flowering are *P.* 'Pandora' which carries shell-pink flowers, while *P.* 'Snow Goose' and *P.* 'Umineko' have white flowers and green new leaves.

P. maackii bears white flowers in short racemes in April, but its best feature is the smooth, yellowish brown, peeling bark. Spreading; 16 × 10 ft (5 × 3 m); 26 × 16 ft (8 × 5 m).

P. sargentii (Sargent cherry) has pink flowers in early April, with the initially wine-coloured new foliage turning brilliant red in September. Spreading; 16 × 13 ft (5 × 4 m); 26 × 23 ft (8 × 7 m).

P. serrula (Tibetan cherry) is grown for the shining, mahogany-coloured, peeling bark. The flowers are small and white, while the leaves are willow-like. Spreading; 16 × 10 ft (5 × 3 m); 23 × 16 ft (7 × 5 m).

P. subhirtella has single rose-pink flowers. 'Autumnalis', the autumn cherry, starts to produce its semi-double pink, fading to white flowers in the autumn and continues in a series of flushes over the winter. Spreading; 13 × 10 ft (4 × 3 m); 20 × 16 ft (6 × 5 m). 'Pendula Rosea' and 'Pendula Rubra' bear rose and deep rose flowers in late March and early April. They are weeping and develop a spreading mushroom-like crown up to 13–16 ft (4–5 m) wide.

The Japanese cherries are a group of small trees of hybrid origin, very decorative in flower, but often less so for the remainder of the year. 'Amanogawa', with shell-pink flowers around the end of April, associates well with tulips. Fastigiate; 16 × 3¼ ft (5 × 1 m); 23 × 6½ ft (7 × 2 m). 'Cheal's Weeping Cherry' has deep pink flowers in early April. Weeping; 10–13 ft (3–4 m) × 13–16 ft (4–5 m). 'Kanzan' carries pink double flowers in early May, when it can look glorious, and the foliage turns bronzy orange in autumn. A young tree, being spiky and erect, can appear rather stark, although when older the branches arch out and down. Generally, it is better enjoyed in your neighbour's garden. Upright, then spreading; 16 × 13 ft (5 × 4 m); 30 × 26 ft (9 × 8 m).

'Pink Perfection' bears double rose-pink flowers,in mid-May. Upright; 16 × 13 ft (5 × 4 m); 20 × 20 ft (6 × 6 m). 'Shimidsu Sakura' has flowers which are pink in bud and open pure white, hanging from the horizontal branches in early May. Spreading; 13–16 ft (4–5 m) × 16–20 ft (5–6 m). 'Tai Haku' (great white cherry) produces the largest flowers of any Japanese cherry, a dazzling white, single and over 2 in. (6 cm) across. The new leaves are deep red and become yellow or orange in autumn. Spreading; 20 × 20 ft (6 × 6 m); 26 × 30 ft (8 × 9 m). (See p.146.)

Pyrus Pear
P. salicifolia 'Pendula' (willow-leaved pear) has silvery willow-like foliage on drooping branches, which arch down and out, and white flowers lost among the leaves. Weeping; 10 × 10 ft (3 × 3 m); 16 × 16 ft (5 × 5 m). (See p.129.)

Quercus Oak
Q. pontica (Armenian oak) has large oval leaves up to 8 in. (20 cm) long, with russet autumn colour. Domed; 10 × 10 ft (3 × 3 m); 16 × 16 ft (5 × 5 m).

Previous page: 'Aurea', a slow-growing golden-leaved cultivar of *Picea orientalis*, is one of the daintiest of the spruces

Rhus Sumach

R. typhina (stag's horn sumach) will easily form a small tree with a little pruning (see p.148). The pinnate leaves with many leaflets give glorious autumn shades of orange, yellow, red and purple, followed by the winter silhouette of the stout hairy branches. Domed; 10 × 10 ft (3 × 3 m); 16 × 20 ft (5 × 6 m).

Robinia Robinias are especially useful for hot, dry or sandy sites, but not water-logged soils. The brittle branches are liable to be broken in exposed situations.

R. kelseyi has graceful pinnate leaves and bright rose-coloured, fragrant flowers in June, followed by bristly pods. Spreading; 10–13 ft × 6½ ft (3–4 × 2 m); 16 × 13 ft (5 × 4 m).

R. pseudoacacia (black locust, false acacia): 'Frisia' is a very distinctive tree with golden yellow foliage. Upright; 26 × 13 ft (8 × 4 m); 39 × 16 ft (12 × 5 m). (See p.131.)

Salix Willows are good for wet situations, although the roots can be a problem if they enter a fractured drain. The trees are valuable for the early catkins.

S. caprea (goat willow, great sallow) bears silvery female catkins – as the well-known pussy willow – or large yellow male ones, in early spring. Upright; 26 × 13 ft (8 × 4 m); 33 × 20 ft (10 × 6 m).

S. daphnoides (violet willow) has one-year-old shoots thickly covered in a waxy bloom, giving a whitish blue effect in winter. Upright; 26 × 16 ft (8 × 5 m); 33 × 20 ft (10 × 6 m).

S. pentandra (bay willow), with glossy green foliage, is unusual among willows in producing the long yellow catkins after the leaves, in June. Upright; 13 × 10 ft (4 × 3 m); 23 × 16 ft (7 × 5 m).

S. purpurea (purple osier) has narrow blue-green leaves. Domed; 13 × 10 ft (4 × 3 m); 16 × 16 ft (5 × 5 m). 'Pendula' is a small weeping form, with long hanging branches on a mound-shaped tree up to 16 ft (5 m) tall. It is the ideal weeping willow for small, and indeed most, gardens. 'Eugenei' is a slender erect form; up to 16 × 6½ ft (5 × 2 m).

Sophora

S. japonica (Japanese pagoda tree): 'Pendula' develops a domed drooping form with highly contorted branches, giving an interesting outline in winter. Weeping; 10 × 10 ft (3 × 3 m); 16 × 16 ft (5 × 5 m). (See opposite.)

Sorbus This large genus includes the rowans, which have pinnate leaves with numerous leaflets, and the whitebeams, which have simple not compound leaves, usually silvery beneath. All thrive on a wide variety of soils and are easily transplanted.

S. aria (whitebeam): 'Lutescens' has brilliant silvery new foliage and white flowers, followed by red berries. (See p.12.) 'Chrysophylla' has yellow leaves throughout the summer. Upright; 16 × 10 ft (5 × 3 m); 26 × 20 ft (8 × 6 m).

S. aucuparia (rowan, mountain ash) has pinnate leaves, white flowers and red berries, which ripen at the beginning of August but are quickly stripped by birds. 'Fructu Luteo' has orange-yellow berries which are less rapidly eaten by birds. Upright; 20 × 13 ft (6 × 4 m); 30 × 20 ft (9 × 6 m).

S. cashmiriana bears pink flowers in May, followed by large white berries like glistening marbles, which last into the winter. Spreading; 13 × 13 ft (4 × 4 m); 20 × 23 ft (6 × 7 m).

S. commixta provides brilliant autumn colour, but does not flower or fruit well. Upright; 23 × 24 ft (7 × 4 m); 33 × 20 ft (10 × 6 m). 'Embley' is a form with glowing red autumn foliage.

Previous page: Prunus subhirtella 'Pendula Rosea', a beautiful small umbrella-like tree, which has been grown in British gardens since the late nineteenth century

The violet willow, *Salix daphnoides*, is worth planting both for the colourful shoots and for the handsome yellow catkins, appearing in March before the leaves

S. folgneri is like a whitebeam with pendulous branches. The leaves turn russet in autumn on the upper surface, contrasting well with the vividly silvery undersides. Spreading; 16 × 10 ft (5 × 3 m); 30 × 20 ft (9 × 6 m).

S. glabrescens has small, shining white fruits, which continue long into the winter, and the leaves display fine red and yellow or orange-yellow colours in late October. Upright; 20 × 10 ft (6 × 3 m); 33 × 16 ft (10 × 5 m). It is usually offered under the name *S. hupehensis*, although the latter is distinguished by pinky berries and kite-shaped sea-green leaves. *S. forrestii* has larger white fruits and the foliage gives good autumn colour. Spreading; 10 × 6½ ft (3 × 2 m); 16 × 16 ft (5 × 5 m). Generally, birds do not touch the berries of white-fruited rowans until well into winter.

S. rehderiana 'Joseph Rock' has amber-yellow berries contrasting with the fiery crimson and purple of the autumn leaves and persisting for several weeks on the bare branches. Upright; 23 × 10 ft (7 × 3 m); 33 × 16 ft (10 × 5 m).

Previous page: The gracefully weeping *Sophora japonica* 'Pendula' has rich green leaves divided into leaflets; it is excellent as a lawn tree or for making an arbour

S. scalaris has bold ladder-like leaves comprising numerous closely set leaflets and gives a long season of interest. The new leaves of dark crimson or bronze expand in April, then white flowers are carried in large dense heads in June, followed by the ripening red berries against the dark, glossy green leaves and finally the rich reds and purples of its autumn colour. Spreading; 13 × 16 ft (4 × 5 m); 20 × 26 ft (6 × 8 m). (See p.124 and p.175.)

S. vilmorinii has leaves composed of many small leaflets, which turn red and purple in autumn. The berries colour maroon or crimson in September and fade through pink to white. Spreading; 10 × 10 ft (3 × 3 m); 16 × 20 ft (5 × 6 m).

S. wardii is a whitebeam with ribbed leaves, grey downy when young, adopting russet colours in autumn. It is sometimes offered as *S. thibetica*, under the collector's number Kingdon Ward 21127. Upright; 13 × 6½ ft (4 × 2 m); 16 × 10 ft (5 × 3 m).

S. thibetica 'John Mitchell' (*S.* 'Mitchellii') has broad, nearly round, leaves, occasionally 8 in. (20 cm) long, bright silver beneath. Domed; 23 × 10 ft (7 × 3 m); 33 × 16 ft (10 × 5 m).

Staphylea Bladder nut

S. holocarpa has leaves consisting of three leaflets and carries panicles of pink flowers in spring on bare branches or with the bronze new foliage. The fruit is a pear-shaped bladder. Upright; 16 × 10 ft (5 × 3 m); 23 × 13 ft (7 × 4 m).

Stuartia

S. pseudocamellia bears single, white, camellia-like flowers with a yellow boss of stamens in August. The bark is attractively flaky, while the leaves in autumn colour purplish, red or yellow. It is better on a moist lime-free soil. Upright; 16 × 10 ft (5 × 3 m); 30 × 16 ft (9 × 5 m).

Styrax

S. japonica (snowbell tree) has widespreading level branches, clothed in June with a mass of hanging bell-shaped flowers, white with yellow stamens. It prefers a moist lime-free soil in a sunny or semi-shaded position. Domed or conical; 10 × 6½ ft (3 × 2 m); 20 × 13 ft (6 × 4 m).

Thuja

T. koraiensis is evergreen and has leaves of matt yellow-green above, conspicuously silver beneath. The foliage has a strong fruity smell, especially when crushed. Upright; 10 × 6½ ft (3 × 2 m); 16 × 10 ft (5 × 3 m).

Tilia Lime, linden

T. mongolica (Mongolian lime) has prominent toothed leaves of glossy green, becoming yellow in autumn, and carries many fragrant small flowers in late July. Domed; 20 × 13 ft (6 × 4 m); 33 × 20 ft (10 × 6 m).

Trachycarpus

T. fortunei (Chusan palm) is an evergreen, which is hardy in southern and western Britain and probably in sheltered locations elsewhere, although young plants need winter protection. It slowly develops a tall trunk, covered with the fibrous bases of the leaves, and bears a cluster of enormous fan-shaped leaves, to nearly 4 ft (120 cm) across. Upright; 5 × 6½ ft (1.5 × 2 m); 10 × 6½ ft (3 × 2 m).

Tsuga Hemlock

T. heterophylla (western hemlock), an evergreen, is graceful as a young tree, with pendulous tips to the leading shoot and branches and dark green needles silvery beneath. It will thrive even in shady situations and on dry, acidic, sandy soils, although eventually growing too tall. Upright; 20 × 10 ft (6 × 3 m); 39 × 16 ft (12 × 5 m).

Previous page: *Sorbus scalaris*, introduced from China in 1904, is a delightful small tree with a short trunk and broad crown
Opposite: After the showy flowers have faded, *Stuartia pseudocamellia* produces brilliant autumn colours from the leaves

Table: trees for specific situations and purposes

Category	Feature	Abies	Acer	Aesculus	Alnus	Aralia	Arbutus	Betula	Calocedrus	Carpinus	Catalpa	Cedrus	Cercidiphyllum	Cercis	Chamaecyparis	Cornus	Corylus	Cotoneaster	Crataegus	Cupressus	Decaisnea	Embothrium
features	ornamental bark		●					●												●		
	flowers	●					●	●				●		●		●	●	●	●	●	●	●
	fruits	●						●								●		●	●	●		
	coloured twigs		●		●																●	
	autumn tints		●					●		●			●			●			●			
foliage	variegated		●													●						
	gold/silver/grey/blue	●	●		●							●			●					●		
	purple		●																			
	coloured when young		●	●									●									
habit	fastigiate									●					●							●
	weeping				●			●				●										
	spreading/domed		●	●			●	●	●		●			●		●	●	●	●			
	upright/conical	●	●	●	●			●	●			●	●		●					●	●	
	deciduous		●	●	●	●		●		●	●		●	●		●	●		●		●	
situation	evergreen	●					●		●			●			●			●		●		●
	coastal		●				●											●	●	●		
	cold exposed		●		●			●	●									●	●	●		
	shade	●	●												●		●					
soil	wet/moist				●			●									●		●		●	●
	dry				●	●	●	●	●	●		●	●	●	●		●	●	●	●		
	chalk	●	●	●		●	●	●	●	●	●	●	●	●	●	●	●	●	●	●	●	

		Eucalyptus	Eucryphia	Euonymus	Fagus	Fraxinus	Genista	Ginkgo	Gleditsia	Halesia	Hydrangea	Ilex	Juniperus	Koelreuteria	Laburnum	Laurus	Ligustrum	Lindera	Magnolia	Mahonia	Malus	Metasequoia	Morus
features	ornamental bark	●																	●			●	
	flowers	●	●			●	●				●	●		●	●	●	●	●	●	●	●		
	fruits			●							●				●						●		●
	coloured twigs																						
	autumn tints			●	●		●	●										●			●	●	
foliage	variegated											●					●						
	gold/silver/grey/blue	●							●			●	●				●						
	purple			●																			
	coloured when young	●																					
habit	fastigiate			●				●					●										
	weeping			●	●							●	●										
	spreading/domed	●		●	●	●			●		●	●	●	●	●		●	●	●	●	●		●
	upright/conical	●	●		●	●	●	●		●				●		●	●		●		●	●	
	deciduous			●	●	●		●	●	●	●			●	●		●	●	●		●	●	●
	evergreen	●	●				●					●	●			●	●		●	●			
situation	coastal	●	●	●	●						●	●	●			●	●		●				
	cold exposed	●		●	●							●	●										
	shade			●	●							●	●										
soil	wet/moist			●	●					●	●							●	●			●	
	dry	●		●	●	●	●	●	●		●	●	●	●	●	●	●				●		●
	chalk	●	●	●	●	●	●	●	●		●	●	●	●	●	●	●		●	●	●	●	●

179

Table: trees for specific situations and purposes

Category	Feature	Nothofagus	Nyssa	Picea	Pinus	Prunus	Pyrus	Quercus	Rhus	Robinia	Salix	Sophora	Sorbus	Staphylea	Stuartia	Styrax	Tilia	Thuja	Trachycarpus	Tsuga
features	ornamental bark				●	●					●				●				●	
features	flowers					●	●			●	●		●	●	●	●	●			
features	fruits					●	●						●	●						
features	coloured twigs										●									
features	autumn tints	●	●			●		●	●				●	●		●				
foliage	variegated																			
foliage	gold/silver/grey/blue			●	●		●			●	●		●					●		●
foliage	purple										●									
foliage	coloured when young	●				●	●			●										
habit	fastigiate					●												●		
habit	weeping					●	●				●	●								●
habit	spreading/domed		●			●	●	●	●	●	●	●	●	●		●	●			
habit	upright/conical	●	●	●	●	●				●	●		●	●	●	●		●	●	●
habit	deciduous	●	●			●	●	●	●	●	●	●	●	●	●	●	●			
habit	evergreen			●	●													●	●	●
situation	coastal			●	●						●		●							
situation	cold exposed	●		●	●						●		●					●		●
situation	shade																	●		●
soil	wet/moist	●	●	●	●		●				●		●		●	●		●		●
soil	dry			●	●	●	●	●		●			●	●				●	●	●
soil	chalk			●	●	●	●	●	●	●	●	●	●	●			●	●	●	●

The Katsura tree, *Cercidiphyllum japonicum*, has small heart-shaped leaves similar to those of the Judas tree, which colour dramatically in autumn

Shrubs for Small Gardens

— KEITH RUSHFORTH —

Dominating this bed is a fragrant white-flowered *Philadelphus* growing with *Cotinus coggygria* 'Royal Purple' and a spiraea

Introduction

This is a guide to the use of shrubs in small gardens. It considers their role and placing in the garden, gives advice on purchase, planting and pruning and finally provides a selection of over 250 suitable shrubs.

Shrubs, if well chosen, have many merits, particularly where the small garden is concerned. Their attractions are not confined to flowers, but include colourful foliage and fruits, decorative bark and distinctive shapes or habits. They can supply interest throughout the seasons, often changing as the year progresses, and once established they require little maintenance, apart from any pruning which may be necessary. Although shrubs may seem expensive to buy, they are a good investment, lasting for at least five years and usually many more. They are also better value than most other plants, relative to the area of garden they occupy.

Shrubs give structure to a garden, associating well with anything from spring bulbs to herbaceous plants and acting as a backcloth to seasonal flowers. They have practical advantages as well, contributing shelter and shade to the garden, screening and separating different areas, filling surplus space and providing homes and food for wildlife.

The definition of a shrub is a low woody plant that does not grow as tall as a tree. For the purposes of this book, which is concerned with small gardens, a shrub can be defined as any woody plant in the height range of 4 in. to 10 ft (10 cm–3 m). Climbers are also included, being especially useful where ground space is scarce.

The size of garden envisaged in this book ranges from the small front and back gardens typical of many new housing estates – perhaps 15–20 by 30 ft (4.5–6 × 9 m) for the back garden – up to more generous plots 50 by 70 ft (15 × 21 m). Even if the overall dimensions of your garden are larger than these, there may still be small areas of garden at the front or side of the house and it is often useful to treat a large garden as a series of smaller spaces. At the other extreme, there is no minimum size of garden needed before shrubs can be introduced. Several of the smaller-growing shrubs can be used just as effectively in containers, such as tubs, half-barrels, old sinks or window boxes, as in a border or bed.

Opposite: The gracefully weeping *Buddleia alternifolia* makes a fine specimen shrub

The Role of Shrubs in a Small Garden

WHERE TO GROW SHRUBS

Shrubs can serve many different purposes, even in a small garden. They can be used individually as feature plants – at the edge of a lawn or patio, for instance, or beside a small pool; or they can form part of a mixed border, providing a background to the herbaceous element when it is at its best and giving substance to the border at other seasons. Dwarf shrubs lend interest and contrast to a rock garden; they may find a place in a raised bed or can be inserted in pockets of soil between the paving stones on a terrace. Dense low shrubs, like heathers and certain hebes, are useful as ground cover and some can be particularly valuable in a shady situation or on a slope which might otherwise be difficult to plant.

All sorts of shrubs are suitable for screening – to disguise a dull wall, break the outline of an ugly building or hide the vegetable plot. Many make excellent informal hedges and boundary-markers, especially those of naturally low growth. Although this type of hedge takes up more room than a closely clipped formal hedge, it offers the attractions of flowers and fruits, as well as foliage, and needs pruning only once a year or less. *Berberis* × *stenophylla*, *Hypericum* 'Hidcote' and *Potentilla fruticosa* are just some that can be recommended for the purpose.

Climbers and wall shrubs recommend themselves in a restricted space, where they can be grown up trellises, fences and walls and add another dimension to the garden. An effective boundary can be created with a climber such as ivy grown over a chain-link fence, making a natural feature that needs less room and maintenance than most hedges. Vigorous climbers can also be trained up trees to give a "second flowering", for example, a summer-flowering clematis grown through a magnolia. As already mentioned, shrubs can also be grown in containers to enliven a patio or small courtyard.

CHOOSING SHRUBS

Because space is limited in a small garden, there will only be room for a finite number of shrubs. Accordingly, careful thought should be given to their selection. The main requirement is that they represent good value for the space they occupy. The criteria for

Above: The cut-leaved Japanese maple, *Acer palmatum* 'Dissectum', provides a long season of interest with its elegant foliage
Below: *Berberis* × *stenophylla* (left) can be used as a delightful informal hedge; *Hedera algeriensis* 'Gloire de Marengo' (right) trained up an old tree stump

choosing any shrub should include not just its obvious attractions of flowers, fruit or foliage, but also its shape, the height and spread it will attain, and how quickly, the pruning and maintenance that will be necessary and its suitability for your conditions, particularly for the position in which you intend to place it. (Information on a wide range of shrubs and their individual needs is given in the final chapter, pp.212–240.) Do not include too many different kinds of shrub in a small garden, as the result will be fussy and cluttered.

GARDEN DESIGN WITH SHRUBS

Correct placing of a shrub or group of shrubs within the garden requires consideration of several factors, namely the scale of the setting, the shape or habit of plant which is appropriate to the setting and the use of foliage, flower and other characteristics within the setting.

Scale

The scale of planting is very important in creating an attractive garden. Scale, however, is a relative term and depends upon the constraints of the site. In a heather bed, for example, the plants are generally flat and low; here scale can be provided with a dwarf conifer or a miniature rowan, *Sorbus reducta*, to break up the monotony and thereby compliment the heathers. At the same time, scale must relate to the surroundings so that the whole planting, not just the individual shrubs, fits in with the space around. Thus, a broad expanse of lawn with a bed of low-growing shrubs at the far end will look odd if these abut the rear garden wall; instead, the planting should lead into or disguise the wall with taller shrubs. A shrub as a focal point in a long narrow garden would generally need to be tall and upright, whereas in a short but broad garden a spreading low shrub would be better balanced.

For obvious reasons, low-growing plants are usually placed at the front of a border, with tall ones at the back. However, nothing looks worse than orderly rows of plants based strictly on height and a better effect can be achieved by planting in informal drifts of varying heights. It may also be visually interesting to have an area of low plants between taller ones, so that the low group can be seen as a feature from one specific point in the garden. Scale is determined by function as well: space might suggest shrubs no taller than 5 ft (1.5 m) for a particular corner, but the need to screen the patio from a neighbour's window or draw the eye away from some distant monstrosity may dictate shrubs of twice that height.

Shape or habit

Shrubs are available in a multitude of shapes, each of which has a part to play in the garden. Three distinctive shapes are discussed below, with suggestions for their use.

Erect-growing or spiky shrubs, such as *Camellia × williamsii*, *Daphne mezereum*, *Hedera helix* 'Conglomerata Erecta' and *Mahonia × media*, are useful specimen plants on their own or can give height at the back of a border or provide a contrast to rounded or weeping shrubs. Many of them can also be trained against a wall.

Mound-forming or arching shrubs strike a restful note. Again, they can be used as individual specimens, perhaps at the edge of a pool or lawn, or included in a border, with the position dependent upon their size. Some may be effective cascading over a low wall. Examples in this category are *Ceanothus impressus*, *Cytisus × praecox*, *Exochorda × macrantha* 'The Bride', *Genista lydia*, *Arundinaria murieliae*, *Buddleia alternifolia* and *Chamaecyparis pisifera* 'Filifera Aurea'.

Low spreading shrubs, like heathers, *Juniperus horizontalis*, *Rhododendron* 'Elisabeth Hobbie' and *R. impeditum*, can be used *en masse* to create an illusion of space. They are excellent for carpeting the ground between taller shrubs and trees or at the front of a border and can help to unify different parts of a small garden.

Shape should always be considered in design, but take care not to over-use the contrasting shapes or they will lose their impact and produce a restless effect. This is particularly true in a small garden, where the essential element of surprise will disappear if more than one or two contrasting plants are used.

When positioning shrubs, it is important to consider their future growth in spread as well as height and to allow them room for development. This will mean planting them some distance apart in a border, which will look very sparse to begin with, although the gaps can be filled with annuals, bulbs and other temporary plants in the early years.

Foliage, flowers, fruit and bark

Most shrubs are chosen for their flowers or foliage and, to a lesser extent, their fruit or bark, since these are the features which catch the eye in the garden centre or in a nursery catalogue. Although

Above: The fragrant flowers of *Daphne mezereum* are welcome in early spring

Below: *Ceanothus* 'Blue Mound' forms a dense dome of evergreen foliage covered with blue flowers in May and June

Above: Many of the brooms, like *Cytisus × kewensis*, are effective at the edge of a low wall

Below: The dwarf *Rhododendron impeditum* gives attractive groundcover

we are all susceptible to the attractions of flowers, floral beauty should not be the sole criterion in choosing a shrub, particularly for a small garden, where it is important that plants should earn their keep and perform for as long as possible. Rather, consider what the whole shrub has to offer and try to see the flowers as the icing on a well-conceived cake, with scale, habit and foliage forming the framework of the overall planting. Foliage, after all, is there for the whole summer in most plants and all the year in evergreens, flowers but for a few days or weeks.

Many shrubs have small leaves, for instance, *Escallonia*, *Hebe* and *Osmanthus*. These dainty-leaved plants are generally the most peaceful, with the mass of foliage providing a background to their own and other flowers and creating a feeling of space, which is especially welcome in a small garden. Shrubs with bolder or larger leaves have an architectural quality, which makes them stand out at a distance, and thus they tend to reduce space so that an area becomes more intimate. Examples include *Viburnum davidii*, with big simple leaves, *Nandina domestica*, with leaves composed of small leaflets, and *Paeonia delavayi*, with deeply dissected leaves. Shrubs with distinctive leaves have a place in the small garden, as accent plants in a mixed border or as impressive features on their own, but they should not be overdone.

Shrubs with evergreen foliage are useful for providing permanent interest. They also make a good backcloth for the display of winter flowers, such as those of *Lonicera fragrantissima*, and supply privacy and shelter. However, all evergreen foliage becomes too dark at some seasons and can be oppressive if there is too much of it. The best effect is when perhaps a quarter to a third of the total number of shrubs is evergreen and these should be distributed throughout the garden rather than forming a solid block.

Variegated shrubs, which have silvery, white or golden margins, splashes or mottlings on the leaves, can help to enliven or break up a planting scheme. *Elaeagnus* × *ebbingei* 'Gilt Edge' is a well-known example. Again, avoid over-using variegated foliage in a small garden and remember that different types of variegation rarely combine well.

There are many shrubs with coloured, as opposed to green leaves, ranging from the copper of *Acer palmatum* 'Bloodgood' and the yellow of *Berberis thunbergii* 'Aurea' to the glaucous-blue of *Abies lasiocarpa* 'Compacta' and the silvery white of *Artemisia* 'Powis Castle'. Grey and silver-leaved shrubs are especially

Opposite: *Berberis thunbergii* 'Aurea' in the garden of Lime Tree Cottage, Weybridge (open under the National Gardens Scheme)

valuable as a foil for other colours. The more strikingly coloured shrubs can be difficult to place and often look better as individual specimens or associated with green- or grey-foliaged plants rather than with each other. Purple-leaved shrubs should be used with particular care if they are not to overwhelm, although they can be lightened with variegated plants.

In several shrubs, the coloured new foliage is an attraction, as with *Pieris formosa* 'Wakehurst' and *Photinia* x *fraseri* 'Red Robin'. In many more, the dying autumn leaves develop beautiful tints, for instance, deciduous azaleas and *Acer palmatum* 'Dissectum', contributing a further dimension to the garden at that time of year. As a bonus, the leaves of a few shrubs, such as *Olearia macrodonta*, release a pleasant aroma, usually when crushed.

A garden without the varied colours, shapes and scents of flowers would be a dull place. There is no doubt that these are the chief attraction of the majority of shrubs and the most conspicuous feature when they are out, even though they are relatively fleeting. In a small garden, shrubs which produce a protracted display, such as *Camellia* x *williamsii*, with a succession of individual blooms, and *Hydrangea paniculata*, with unusually long-lasting flowers, are especially desirable. By careful selection, it is possible to have a shrub in flower every month of the year. Winter-flowering shrubs are always appreciated and many of them, like *Mahonia* x *media*, fill the air with their rich perfume.

Several shrubs have decorative fruit, which is also valuable in the autumn and winter period and sometimes at other seasons. The silky seedheads of *Clematis alpina* 'Frances Rivis' and the large hips of *Rosa rugosa* 'Fru Dagmar Hastrup', for example, both appear from July on, while the berries of some cotoneasters persist until Easter. Bark is largely a winter feature, being hidden by foliage at other times. It is best displayed when the shrub is cut back hard in early spring, as with the forms of *Cornus alba*, in which the one-year-old twigs are brightly coloured. The peeling bark of shrubs like *Cistus laurifolius* and *Weigela middendorffiana* is also attractive.

Shrubs grown for winter effect, whether bark, fruit or flowers, should be placed where they can be seen from inside or near the front door or a much-used path if they are scented, otherwise they may easily be missed until you venture out into the garden again in spring!

Above: 'St Ewe', one of the many valuable *Camellia × williamsii* forms, flowers over a long period

Below: *Spiraea japonica* 'Gold Flame' has delicately coloured young foliage

Above: The brilliantly coloured berries of *Pernettya mucronata* 'Cherry Ripe' remain throughout the winter

Below: The dogwoods, such as *Cornus stolonifera* 'Flaviramea', make a striking contribution to the winter scene

Practical Considerations

Successful gardening involves knowing the limitations of your site, as well as its good points, and taking these into account when planning and planting. Not all shrubs like or tolerate the same conditions and an appreciation of their individual preferences can make the difference between a garden where you have time to sit back and enjoy the display and one where every blossom is gained only after a marathon effort. (Guidance on soil, light, hardiness, pruning and any other requirements is given in the selection of shrubs, pp.212–240.) This chapter looks at the factors affecting your choice of shrubs, with particular reference to the problems associated with small gardens.

SOIL

Very few gardens possess the ideal soil – a good loam – and the type of soil may place a constraint upon what will grow or reduce its rate of growth. Fortunately, most shrubs are accommodating plants, only a small number having definite dislikes, and it is possible to find a shrub to suit almost every soil.

Rhododendrons and many heathers and their relatives will not grow on soils derived from chalk or limestone. Giving nutrients in a chelated form may assist where the soil is only slightly alkaline, but in the long run it is better to choose from the many shrubs which grow freely on these soils rather than struggle to get healthy rhododendrons. Similarly, acid soils impose restrictions on what will succeed and, although they can be improved by liming, it is wiser to select from the numerous shrubs available which thrive in such soils.

Clay soils are difficult for shrubs to root through and poorly drained. They also tend to take time to warm up in spring, causing plants to be late in starting into growth and slow to grow, especially when young. They can be improved by working in organic matter and by digging them in autumn to let frost break down the clods. Surface water should be drained away with pipes, or the border shaped into mounds to give sufficient rooting depth. Avoid walking on clay soils when they are wet, as this destroys the structure, reducing it to a formless mass which is impenetrable to plant roots.

Sandy soils, by contrast, are very free-draining, drying out quickly in the summer, and hold little in the way of nutrients,

although plants can root readily through them. They can be improved by adding organic matter, such as peat or well-rotted manure, which will increase their capacity for retaining water and nutrients.

Problems of the soil, or lack of it, are common in small gardens. Many town gardens suffer from dry impoverished soil, particularly where there is heavy shade. Thorough preparation of the soil, by digging and incorporating plenty of humus is essential. Compaction, which prevents roots penetrating the soil and water draining away, is often found in new gardens where heavy machinery has been used during house construction. Sometimes the whole layer of topsoil may have been removed as well. Digging to two spade depths (see p.204) is the most practical method to relieve compaction in a small garden and it may also be necessary to buy in extra top soil.

Closely packed soil may lead to waterlogging or very wet conditions, which few plants can survive. Installing drainage is the best way to improve such a soil, but it will only work if there is somewhere for the water to drain away. If this is not possible, plant on mounds or choose shrubs like *Cornus alba* that will tolerate wetness.

CLIMATE

Although there is considerable variation in climate over the length of Britain, it is surprising how many shrubs will thrive throughout the country. However, some shrubs are only reliably hardy in the milder parts of southern and western Britain. This applies to many hebes, for example and there is little point trying them in colder districts unless they can be given suitable protection. Other shrubs, lilac, for instance, do better in the eastern counties, although they will grow elsewhere. Town gardens usually benefit from higher temperatures in winter than the suburbs and countryside, owing to the heat escaping from houses and offices. As a result, less hardy shrubs can often be grown, especially against walls, and camellias are particularly successful in towns.

Like camellias, a number of shrubs are vulnerable to late spring frosts, either because the flowers are pre-formed in buds made the previous year or because they have early flowers whose petals are easily damaged. If the new growth is injured by frost, that season's flowering may be lost. Shrubs of this kind (noted in the

Opposite: *Syringa microphylla* 'Superba' and other lilacs will thrive on alkaline soils

Above: The magnificent *Desfontainea spinosa* does best in warm moist conditions and lime-free soil

Below: The Mexican orange blossom, *Choisya ternata*, is tough enough for seaside gardens

last chapter, pp.212–240, as needing some protection) should be positioned in the garden so that they are not in frost pockets and, if possible, sheltered from the early morning sun to reduce the risk of damage. The alternatives are either to choose frost-hardier shrubs, or to accept the fact that every now and then frost might mar the display.

Exposure to winds influences the growth rate and appearance of all plants, not only causing physical damage but also drying out the foliage and soil. Turbulence from buildings is a frequent problem in towns. Planting a windbreak or making a screen can be a solution, if there is room. Otherwise, tough plants, such as *Cornus alba*, *Cotinus coggygria*, *Euonymus fortunei* cultivars, *Hydrangea paniculata*, heathers and *Pernettya mucronata*, should be chosen where wind exposure is severe.

Coastal gardens tend to be windier than those inland, with nothing to reduce the wind speed as it comes off the sea, and salt spray adds to the damage. In these situations, it is advisable to select salt-resistant shrubs, which include *Choisya ternata*, *Cotoneaster*, *Cytisus*, *Escallonia*, *Euonymus*, *Hebe*, *Olearia*, *Rhamnus alaterna* and *Senecio*.

ASPECT

Shrubs vary in their light requirements. Many grow best in an open sunny position, where they receive from four to six hours daily of direct sunlight in summer (described as "sun" in the list of shrubs, pp.212–240). A small number need more sun, really wanting a hot dry site with as much sunlight as possible in our climate (noted as "full sun" in the list). These are mainly members of the pea family, such as *Genista* and *Cytisus*, and can be useful in small enclosed gardens where there is often a hot dry spot, perhaps at the foot of a south-facing wall.

Other shrubs tolerate or prefer light shade, where they receive less than four hours direct sunlight each day; an open north-facing bed or wall would be in this category. Permanent heavy shade, which is a common feature in small gardens overlooked by taller buildings or trees, is more difficult to deal with. Nevertheless, there are several shrubs such as *Mahonia × media*, *Viburnum davidii* and *Euonymus fortunei*, that will accept deep shade.

Choosing the right shrub for the level of shade is important: those needing full sun will be weedy and at best flower very poorly if in shade, whereas many shade-loving shrubs, like some rhododendrons, will not be happy in full sun. (See also the Wisley Handbook, *Plants for Shade*.)

Above: The distinctive flowers of *Ribes speciosum*, borne in April and May, are vulnerable to late frosts

Below: *Convolvulus cneorum*, a charming shrub for a hot dry position

Purchase and Planting

TYPES OF SHRUB AVAILABLE

Shrubs are usually purchased as bare-rooted, root-balled or container-grown plants. Bare-rooted shrubs are grown in open fields in a nursery and, when they are lifted, all the soil is shaken off; the roots are then wrapped in some material, such as damp straw, to prevent then drying out. Many deciduous shrubs may be bought bare-rooted, for planting during the winter season from November until March. Because they are grown in the field, larger sizes are often available.

Evergreens rarely survive with bare roots, but can be moved with a root ball, which involves keeping the soil attached to the roots and wrapping them in hessian. Root-balled shrubs can be planted out earlier in the autumn and into April.

Container-grown shrubs are put into a pot one or more years before being sold. As a result, they should not suffer any check from loss of roots on lifting and can be planted at times other than during the winter planting season. Most shrubs from garden centres are container-grown for this reason, allowing them to be sold and planted at any time of the year. Another advantage is that evergreens and shrubs with thick fleshy roots, such as magnolias, can be planted more safely if container-grown, even during the winter.

The main risk with a container-grown shrub is that it may have become pot-bound and, when planted, will not form a satisfactory new root system in the different environment of the soil. This can happen when the shrub has spent too long in a container and the roots are growing round the pot, which they will continue to do, rather than spreading out into the soil. Container-grown shrubs are also more expensive than bare-rooted plants and in hard winters the roots can be killed in the containers, leading to failure in the spring.

BUYING SHRUBS

Shrubs can be purchased from reputable nurseries by mail order (or in person), from garden centres and from plant sales areas attached to gardens open to the public, the latter often stocking more unusual shrubs. Generally, bare-rooted shrubs should be bought and planted only during the period November to early

The popular *Magnolia stellata* carries a profusion of flowers in March and April

March, while container-grown shrubs can be bought at other times. However, it is wise to avoid the midsummer months, July and early August, when they will be growing vigorously and a lot of attention to watering will be necessary. Slightly tender shrubs are best planted in late spring; for other shrubs, autumn planting is usually preferable, but not always as convenient.

PLANTING

Planting will vary a little according to whether you are making a new bed or border or replacing plants in an existing one. With a new bed, the outline should be marked out and perennial weeds should be killed with a herbicide like glyphosate, which does not persist in the soil, taking care to avoid any cultivated plants. This is best carried out in September, but can be done at any time when the weeds are actively growing. Once the weeds are dead, the ground should be well dug, or dug to two spade depths if there is any sign of soil compaction (the top spit of soil is removed and put to one side and then the second spit is turned over with a spade before replacing the topsoil). Autumn is the recommended time for digging, especially on heavy soils, and the soil can be left over winter to let the action of frost break it down. Organic matter, such as peat or well-rotted manure, can be spread over the bed before digging and thus incorporated.

The first stage in planting is to excavate a hole, which should be dug at least 4 in. (10 cm) larger in each direction than the spread of the shrub's roots or the size of the container. If planting into an existing bed, the bottom and sides of the hole should be forked over, so that the roots can easily grow out. Soil should then be placed back in the hole until it is as deep as the depth of the roots, but no deeper. Peat or potting compost can be mixed with the soil and this is advisable for container-grown shrubs, as the compost in the pot will contain peat. Do not attempt to plant if the ground is frozen solid or covered with snow, but keep the shrub in a cool place until the weather is suitable.

The roots of a bare-rooted shrub should be spread out in the hole and soil worked between them, consolidating it in layers with the feet, but being careful not to stamp on the roots. The final soil level should be at the nursery soil level, which will show as a dark mark on the stems or bark. If some roots are badly damaged, the damaged parts can be cut out, but as far as possible avoid further reducing the roots.

Before planting a container-grown shrub, give it a good soak in a bucket of water for five to ten minutes. This is especially important when planting in summer, but even in mid-winter the compost in a container can easily dry out. Bare-rooted plants will also benefit from a brief soaking if they are dry. With a container-grown shrub, the roots may be circling the bottom of the pot and they should either be teased out or the surface spiral of roots cut at three points, cutting no deeper into the compost than $\frac{3}{4}$ in. (1 cm), so that new spreading roots are formed. If the plant is pot-bound, with very woody circling roots, it should be returned to the supplier. Then proceed as with a bare-rooted shrub, again planting no deeper than the soil surface level of the container.

Root-balled shrubs should be placed in the hole and the hessian untied and cut away at the sides. Do not attempt to remove it from beneath the root ball, or you will damage this and reduce its effectiveness; the hessian will rot away.

After planting, the shrub should be watered, using at least 2 gallons (9 litres) water per plant. In late spring and summer, the same amount of water will have to be given once a week or more for a month and you should keep an eye open for any sign of wilting. A few days after planting and after windy weather, check that the soil around the roots has not been loosened and firm it if necessary. Most shrubs will not require any staking, but if they do, bamboo canes should be used, attaching the shrub to the cane with tape.

WEED CONTROL

The first requirement with any newly planted shrub is to get it to grow strongly. Provided proper care has been taken with the actual planting, this is best achieved by thorough weed control for at least the first two seasons after planting. Grasses and clovers are the worst weeds from the point of view of their effect upon shrubs, since they compete fiercely for water and nutrients. Other broad-leaved weeds are much less of a problem, although they can be very unsightly. Spring bulbs and annuals can be used to fill the gaps between shrubs and are unlikely to harm them, but vigorous ground-covering perennials like *Geranium* should be avoided for the first couple of seasons.

Starting with a weed-free bed (see p.204) is essential to satisfactory weed control. Subsequent weed invasion is best controlled by using a long-lasting mulch. Composted conifer bark is highly recommended for the purpose and will last for three to five years. It is available in bags from garden centres or sometimes in bulk at a lower price from local landscape contractors. Various other forms of organic matter can also be used, but do not persist as long. In certain situations, pea gravel, around $\frac{3}{4}$ in. (1 cm) in diameter, can make a very satisfactory mulch. Sheeting materials, such as 500 gauge black polythene, are very effective too, although unattractive in a garden. However, porous sheeting materials can be useful as a layer beneath the mulch to prevent it being worked into the soil – even gravel becomes incorporated into the soil by the action of worms. Some mulches can be helpful in providing food, particularly manure, spent hops and mushroom compost. The latter has a high pH and is therefore unsuitable for acid-loving shrubs. Bark does not add nutrients, although all organic mulches will increase the humus content of the soil and help to improve its structure.

A mulch must be spread thickly enough to prevent weeds germinating through it, to a depth of at least 2 in. (5 cm) and preferably 4 in. (10 cm) (except with sheet materials). The ground should be free of perennial weeds, such as couch grass and ground elder, before the mulch is laid; these are best killed with glyphosate when in active growth. The mulch is best applied in spring, when the ground is moist and is beginning to warm up.

Herbicides are another method of controlling weeds in shrub

With shiny evergreen leaves, fragrant flowers and bright red berries,
Skimmia japonica 'Foremanii' has everything to recommend it

beds and borders. Dichlobenil can be used around most trees and
shrubs when well established. It is soil-acting, persisting for
several months. Foliage-acting glyphosate can be used as a careful
spot-treatment during the growing season. Always take particular
care not to overdose and to avoid the chemicals coming in contact
with the shrubs or other ornamental plants. When using
herbicides, follow the recommendations given by the
manufacturer on the label.

WATERING

Weed control and mulching will reduce the need for watering, by
limiting competition for moisture and by restricting water loss
through evaporation from the soil. However, in very dry periods
and with newly planted shrubs, some extra watering may be
necessary. Potentially, a shrub bed can lose the equivalent of
roughly 1 in. (2.5 cm) of rainfall a week during June and July, $\frac{3}{4}$ in.
(2 cm) in May and August and $\frac{1}{2}$ in. (1 cm) in April and September.
If there has not been this amount of rain, the missing water should
be replaced, preferably with a sprinkler applied to the whole bed.

Hibiscus syriacus 'Diana' (left), a recently introduced form from the USA; the calico bush, *Kalmia latifolia* (right), flourishes in the same conditions as rhododendrons

FEEDING

In most garden situations, shrubs will not require feeding, although it may enhance growth. Well-rotted manure or compost can be used as part of the mulch or as a top dressing, or a chemical fertilizer can be applied. Do not over-feed, as this may poison the shrubs. A general-purpose fertilizer, with an analysis of around 7 to 10 parts each of nitrogen, phosphorus and potassium, is suitable, at a rate of 2 oz per square yard (70 gm per m^2). With all shrubs, it is especially important to apply any feed to bare earth. If grass or other weeds are present, they and not the shrub will make the increased growth, which could lead to a reduction in the growth of the shrub owing to the competition.

PESTS AND DISEASES

Although shrubs can be affected by a variety of pests and diseases, these are seldom serious. Aphids, which may occasionally be a problem, can be easily controlled with a proprietary insecticide, if possible using one which does not kill ladybirds and other insect predators of aphids. Fungal diseases, such as honey fungus, caused by species of *Armillaria*, can be extremely damaging and, if symptoms are suspected, it is wise to seek expert advice. (For further information, see the *Collins Guide to the Pests, Diseases and Disorders of Garden Plants* by Stefan Buczacki and Keith Harris.)

Pruning

Pruning has three main objectives – to control the size and shape of a shrub, to keep it healthy and to enhance its beauty.

CONTROL AND SHAPING

Pruning to control size is necessary when a shrub is growing too large for its location. The aim is to reduce its size without just hacking it back; if the offending branches are simply lopped off, regrowth is likely to be more vigorous and may quickly cause as much trouble as the portion removed. Prune by cutting the longer branches back to a suitable and smaller sideshoot, which will retain the original shape of the shrub and keep it in a flowering and fruiting stage.

When shrubs are seriously overgrown, pruning back to side branches may not be sufficient and they may respond to being coppiced, that is, cut down to near ground level. This technique may also be effective at invigorating those in poor health (although if a fungal disease at the roots is the reason for the condition, it is unlikely to be successful). With most shrubs, the new growth made after coppicing is unlikely to flower for two to three years. This hard pruning should normally be carried out in the dormant season or after flowering for deciduous shrubs and in early spring for evergreens like camellias.

MAINTAINING HEALTH

Pruning for health is a matter of removing weak, damaged, dead or overcrowded shoots, in order to prevent or restrict the entry of disease and to eliminate places where damaging insects can hide. Promptly remove any dying branch as soon as it is noticed, by cutting it off at the base. Any branches which are crossing or rubbing together should also be removed. Suckers on grafted shrubs (representing the rootstock, not the desired form) should be removed at their point of origin. With suckers from the roots, the simplest method is to pull the sucker while levering a spade between it and the stem. On variegated shrubs, branches sometimes revert to pure green and these too should be cut out before they take over.

209

Above: Flowering on the previous season's shoots, *Buddleia globosa* (left) and *Clematis alpina* 'Frances Rivis' (right) may be pruned after flowering

Below: Deutzias, like *D. × rosea* 'Carminea', are best pruned every three or four years

ENHANCING BEAUTY

The method and timing of pruning for decorative effect will vary, depending upon how the flowers or other attractive features, such as leaves or bark, are produced. Deciduous shrubs can be divided into two categories – those which flower on last summer's shoots and those which flower on the current season's shoots. Knowing to which group a shrub belongs is important, since different species in one genus may respond very differently. For example, *Buddleia globosa* and *Clematis alpina* are in the first category, while *Buddleia davidii* and *Clematis vernayi* are in the second.

Shrubs flowering on shoots grown last year should be pruned immediately after flowering, which is generally in spring and early summer. The older shoots are removed at the point of origin, encouraging young shoots to replace them in the framework of the bush. The number of young shoots may need to be thinned out at the same time to keep the shrub compact. Many shrubs in this class, for instance *Deutzia* and *Kolkwitzia*, actually flower better on the spur shoots produced on three- or four-year-old shoots; in their case, the pruning regime should be to remove shoots every three or four years. If the fruits as well as the flowers are a feature, as in *Berberis* × *stenophylla*, prune the shrub more lightly.

Shrubs which flower on the current season's shoots are mostly summer- and early autumn-flowering and can be hard pruned in March to give a better display later. Examples are *Buddleia davidii, Ceratostigma willmottianum, Hypericum* 'Hidcote' and *Indigofera heterantha*. If left unpruned, they will usually flower earlier in the summer, but with smaller blooms.

Shrubs like *Cornus alba*, which are grown for the strongly coloured bark of the one-year-old shoots, and some foliage shrubs, such as *Artemisia*, can be treated in the same way to make the most of their attractive features.

Evergreen shrubs, on the whole, require no pruning, except to remove any damaged growth or reverted shoots and to keep them trim and shapely. This should be carried out in late May or early June.

Many other shrubs will give an attractive display without regular pruning, although they will benefit from the removal of dead, diseased or overcrowded shoots. (For further guidance, see the Wisley Handbook, *Pruning Ornamental Shrubs*.)

A Selection of Shrubs for ────── Small Gardens

This chapter contains brief descriptions of over 250 shrubs suitable for small gardens. Most of them have been selected on the basis that they are reliable in gardens throughout the British Isles and are readily available from local garden centres or from the larger national nurseries; a few are less common or may need some extra attention. In many cases, the featured shrub is one of several similar plants and it is only possible to mention one or two of them, as for example with the numerous forms of *Camellia × williamsii*. Space does not allow discussion of more than a sample of available shrubs and the final selection inevitably has a personal bias. However, all have been chosen for their value in a small garden and their ability to contribute something more than just a short burst of bloom.

The information given for each shrub includes its likely height and spread after ten years, in average conditions, what aspect it prefers and any special requirements such as soil or pruning; where there is no reference to these, it can be assumed that any soil is suitable and that no pruning is necessary. If the shrub is evergreen, this is noted, otherwise it is deciduous.

The shrubs, including climbers, are grouped according to their flowering season, from early spring to late summer, followed by sections on autumn and winter effect and year-round interest. All have been selected for more than one attribute and there is therefore some overlap of categories, with many of the flowering shrubs having attractive foliage or fruits and vice-versa. (For further information about particular groups, see the following titles in the Wisley Handbook series – *Climbing and Wall Plants*; *Ground Cover Plants*; *Camellias*; *Clematis*; *Heaths and Heathers*; *Rhododendrons* and *Roses*. See also the earlier section in this book on *Trees for Small Gardens*.)

EARLY SPRING FLOWERS – LATE FEBRUARY TO EARLY APRIL

Abeliophyllum distichum Bare twigs covered with pale bluish pink flowers scented of almonds. Plant against a south- or west-facing wall in sun. Grows to 5 ft (1.5 m) tall and wide. Prune by removing old shoots after flowering.

Camellia × williamsii Large evergreen shrub, 10–16½ by 6½ ft (3–5 × 2 m), but can be controlled by pruning after flowering. Preferable to the more usual *C. japonica*,

Above: *Chaenomeles × superba* 'Pink Lady' (left), with its spreading horizontal branches, is particularly suitable for a wall; *Corylopsis pauciflora* (right) flowers reliably each year, in the right situation, and deserves to be more widely grown

as the cerise-pink flowers are carried in successive flushes from February until May, are more frost-hardy and drop the petals once over. Will grow in full sun but better in light shade. Avoid alkaline soils. 'Donation', semi-double flowers. 'St Ewe', single but effective flowers (see p.195).

Chaenomeles × superba (japonica)   Good for walls or open ground, forming a dense domed bush, 3–5 by 5 ft (1–1.5 × 1.5 m). Flowering from March into May, followed by edible "quince" fruits. Prune after flowering to remove old wood. Sun or light shade. 'Crimson and Gold', crimson petals and contrasting gold anthers. 'Knaphill Scarlet', large, brilliant red flowers. 'Pink Lady', flowers crimson in bud, opening to rose-pink.

Corylopsis pauciflora   Scented primrose-yellow flowers on bare branches in March. Makes a rounded bush, 3–5 by 3 ft (1–1.5 × 1 m). Site to protect from early morning sun and wind.

Daphne mezereum (mezereon)   Purplish red, fragrant flowers along erect branches, succeeded by poisonous red berries in July. A short-lived bush, 3 by 2 ft (1 × 0.6 m). Full sun to light shade. Any moist soil (see p.190).

D. odora 'Aureomarginata'   Evergreen with leaves margined creamy white, forming rounded bush, 4 by 5 ft (1.2 × 1.5 m). Flowers fragrant, purplish red. Sun or light shade.

Rhododendron   All require acid soil rich in organic matter; never plant deeply and mulch with peat, leafmould or conifer bark. Larger growing sorts should be dead-headed, removing faded flowers before seed is set, to encourage next season's blooms. Dwarf kinds will take full sun if the soil is sufficiently moist, taller ones are better in dappled shade.

R. pemakoense   Develops into a very dense, low, evergreen bush, 1 by 2 ft (0.3 × 0.6 m), with small, dark green leaves. Flowers single or in pairs, completely covering the plant. Place where early morning sun will not catch it, as the flowers are tender.

Spiraea thunbergii   Twiggy bush, 3–5 by 5 ft (1–1.5 × 1.5 m), with arching habit. Small, pure white flowers on leafless twigs, followed by fresh green, new foliage. Full sun (see p.214).

Above: The well-known *Spiraea thunbergii* succeeds in ordinary soil and a sunny spot

Below: *Berberis darwinii* will grow on chalky soils

Stachyurus chinensis Grows to 6 by 6½ ft (1.8 × 2 m). Cup-shaped pale yellow flowers hang beneath arching leafless shoots. Sun or light shade. 'Magpie', grey-green leaves margined with cream and with a rose-coloured tinge.

LATE SPRING FLOWERS – APRIL TO MAY

Berberis candidula Dense dome-shaped evergreen, 2½ by 3 ft (0.8 × 1 m). Glossy green leaves with a silver-blue reverse and solitary, bright yellow flowers succeeded by purple-black berries. Full sun to light shade.

B. darwinii Spectacular when in full flower, with short drooping clusters of 10 to 12 blossoms, in bud deep reddish orange, opening to deep yellow. Berries plum-coloured with waxy coating in autumn, often accompanied by a second small flush of bloom. Evergreen, having deep glossy green leaves with three small prickles. Upright habit, usually up to 5 ft (1.8 m) high, but occasionally taller, by 6½ ft (2 m). Responds to pruning. Full sun or light shade. Can be damaged by severe cold in exposed situations.

B. × stenophylla Evergreen narrow-leaved shrub, 6½–10 ft (2–3 m) high, with graceful habit. Golden yellow flowers carried beneath the arching branches of last season's growth, followed by massed blue-purple fruits. Makes a very effective semi-formal hedge. Trimmed once a year after flowering, new growths will be 2–3 ft (0.6–1 m) long and will flower next spring. Full sun or light shade (see p.187).

Ceanothus (Californian lilac) The spring-flowering kinds, usually evergreen (as are those below), require very little pruning. Should be given a sheltered sunny position, many being recommended as wall shrubs, and will not flourish on shallow soils over chalk.

C. 'A.T. Johnson' Grows 5–10 ft (1.5–3 m) tall. Rich blue flowers borne in both spring and autumn.

C. impressus Low spreading plant, 3–5 ft (1–1.5 m) high and across, with deep blue flowers which smother the small veined leaves.

C. thyrsiflorus var. repens Hardy variety which retains a low prostrate shape, ultimately 3 by 6½–10 ft (1 × 2–3 m). Mid-blue flowers, set off by glossy foliage.

Choisya ternata (Mexican orange blossom) Slow-growing evergreen, 10–13 ft (3–4 m) high, but will withstand cutting back. Leaves consist of three leaflets and are aromatic if crushed. White flowers strongly scented of orange blossom, carried mainly in spring and autumn. Prune to control shape and lightly after the spring flush of flowers for better autumn blossom. Full sun to light shade. Needs a sheltered position in cold districts (see p.200). 'Sundance', with golden foliage, promises to be smaller growing and is best in light shade.

Clematis alpina 'Frances Rivis' Low climber, 6½ by 6½–13 ft (2 × 2–4 m), with violet-blue flowers and deeply divided leaves. The silky seedheads are attractive from July on. Prune only to control spread, since flowers are formed on last season's shoots. Sun or light shade (see p.210).

Cytisus (broom) Short-lived but very floriferous, with pea-like flowers. They grow in all well-drained soils, but must have full sun. The small leaves are soon lost and slender green twigs give the effect of leaves. Brooms do not like any pruning, although shoots can be shortened successfully if they are still green below the point of the cut.

C. × beanii Deep golden yellow flowers in sprays up to 12 in. (30 cm) long from last year's growths. A low semi-prostrate plant, 1½ by 3–5 ft (1–1.5 m). Best replaced every three to four years (see p.216).

C. × kewensis Procumbent shrub, 8 in. by 5 ft (20 cm × 1.5 m), with creamy yellow flowers (see p.191).

C. × praecox Flowers rich cream to sulphur-yellow. Mounded habit with arching shoots, 3–5 ft by 5–6½ ft (1–1.5 × 1.5–2 m).

A superb combination of deep yellow *Cytisus* × *beanii* and purple aubrieta (left) at the National Trust property, Polesden Lacey, in Surrey; the fast-growing *Daphne* × *burkwoodii* (right) appreciates a well-drained soil

---

Daphne × burkwoodii Semi-evergreen bush, 3 ft (1 m) tall and across, with pale pink, sweetly scented flowers. Sun or light shade.

Exochorda × macrantha 'The Bride' Forms a low mound, to 2½–3 by 5 ft (0.8 × 1.5 m). Massed, pure white flowers with large papery petals contrast well with the fresh green, new leaves. Sun or light shade.

Magnolia stellata Dwarf rounded shrub, usually only 3 ft (1m) high and wide, but with time capable of attaining 10–13 by 6½–10 ft (3–4 × 2–3 m). Fragrant, pure white flowers with strap-like petals are carried on bare branches. The petals are easily bruised by frost, so shelter the plant from early morning sun. Sun or light shade (see p.204).

Osmanthus delavayi Small, stiff, glossy green, evergreen leaves hidden by an abundance of very fragrant, pure white flowers. Slow growing, in ten years 3 by 2¼ ft (1 × 0.7 m), but may if unpruned attain 10–20 ft (3–6 m). Prune to control shape as required after flowering. Sun to reasonably deep shade. O. × *burkwoodii*, more vigorous and hardier in cold districts.

Paeonia delavayi (peony) Suckering shrub, 3–5 ft (1–1.5 m) high and wide. Large single flowers, varying from yellow to crimson and, in the best forms, deep blood-red with golden anthers. Handsome, deeply dissected leaves up to 1¼ ft (0.4 m) long. Sun. Any well-drained soil.

Pieris taiwanensis The best pieris for flowers, being loaded with racemes of pure white urn-shaped blooms held horizontally. New foliage is bronze-coloured. Makes a small, rounded, evergreen bush, 3–5 ft (1–1.5 m) tall and across. Prune only occasionally to control shape. Light shade. Acid soils only.

Prunus tenella 'Fire Hill' Dwarf almond forming a spreading bush with erect stems, 4 ft (1.2 m) high and wide. Last year's shoots carry masses of rosy red flowers. Sun or light shade.

Rhododendron 'Bluebird' Compact evergreen, 1½ ft (0.5 m) tall and across, with many rich violet-blue flowers hiding small, fragrant, somewhat yellowish green leaves (see also *Rhododendron*, p.213, for cultivation requirements).

R. calostrotum 'Gigha' Rounded evergreen bush, 2–3 × 3 ft (0.6–1 × 1 m), with small grey-green leaves. Covers itself with deep claret-red flowers.

216

'Elizabeth' (left), one of the finest smaller rhododendron hybrids, was raised at Bodnant in North Wales; the lovely red flower buds of *Viburnum carlesii* 'Diana' (right) are borne throughout winter before opening in spring

R. 'Elizabeth' Spreading evergreen, 3 by 4 ft (1 × 1.2 m), taller in shade, with large scarlet bell flowers and medium green leaves. Protect from early morning sun. R. 'Elisabeth Hobbie' and R. 'Scarlet Wonder', similar, but lower.

R. impeditum Domed dwarf bush, 1 by 1½ ft (0.3 × 0.5 m), which will knit together to give effective evergreen groundcover. Tiny fragrant grey-green leaves, bronze over winter. Flowers pale purplish blue (see p.191).

R. williamsianum Choice mound-forming evergreen, 3 by 6½ ft (1 × 2 m). Rounded leaves flushed bronze and maturing to dark green with a glaucous underside. Flowers, raised above the dense foliage, are soft rosy red bells 2 in. (5 cm) in diameter.

Ribes speciosum Ornamental gooseberry, nearly evergreen, spiny and open branched, 5 ft (1.5 m) high and wide. Exquisite fuchsia-like red flowers hang beneath spreading shoots; these can be hit by late frosts. Prune by removing older shoots after flowering. Sun or light shade (see p.202).

Skimmia japonica Evergreen growing to 3 by 4 ft (1 × 1.2 m), whose glossy leaves are aromatic when crushed. Grown for the very fragrant flowers, particularly on male plants such as 'Rubella', and for the large red berries, produced on female plants like 'Foremanii' when the two sexes are grown together. In 'Rubella', the flower buds are red, giving the bush a reddish hue over winter, and open to pink. Sun or light shade (see p.207).

Spiraea 'Arguta' Rounded bush, 6½ ft (2 m) tall and wide. Pure white flowers on twiggy shoots of previous summer. Prune by removing old shoots. Sun.

Viburnum carlesii 'Diana' Slowly develops a rounded, somewhat open habit, 5 ft (1.5 m) tall and across. Richly scented flowers borne in clusters formed the previous autumn, red in bud, opening to pale pink. Sun or light shade.

Weigela middendorffiana Grows to 4 by 2½ ft (1.2 × 0.8 m) and has a buff-coloured bark. Flowers sulphur-yellow flecked with orange. Requires some shelter against spring frosts in cold gardens. Prune to remove old shoots after flowering. Sun or light shade.

EARLY SUMMER FLOWERS – LATE MAY TO JUNE

Buddleia alternifolia   Spreading, with weeping branches and shoots of the previous summer clothed with dense clusters of lilac-purple, tubular, fragrant flowers. Often recommended as a small weeping tree trained on to a single stem, eventually 10–20 ft (3–6 m) tall. However, if pruned immediately after flowering, to shape and remove old wood, a shrub 3–5 ft (1–1.5 m) high will result. Leaves dull green and glaucous beneath, silvery in 'Argentea' (see p.184).

B. globosa   Golden yellow, sweetly scented flowers in small rounded orange-like heads and long, matt green, lance-shaped leaves, evergreen except in severe winters. Makes an open rounded bush 10–13 ft (3–4 m) high and will regrow vigorously from cutting back; normal pruning should consist only of removing crowded old branches when flowering has ceased. Full sun (see p.210).

Ceanothus 'Blue Mound'   Dense domed evergreen 2 ft (0.6 m) tall, with mid-blue flowers (see p.190 and also *Ceanothus*, p.215, for cultivation requirements).

Clematis chrysocoma   Soft pink flowers in prodigious number, with an intermittent flush from August on. A climber to 26 ft (6 m), but can be cut back hard after flowering in early summer and allowed to clamber over medium-sized shrubs without smothering them. Sun to light shade.

Convolvulus cneorum   Shrubby bindweed, but not at all invasive, which must have a sheltered, rather dry position in full sun to flourish. Evergreen bush, 2 by 2½ ft (0.6 × 0.8 m), with a silvery appearance owing to silky hairs on the leaves. Large trumpet flowers, white tinged with pink with a yellow base, carried into August. Prune to remove untidy shoots in spring. Any well-drained soil (see p.202).

Deutzia   Reliable shrubs with fragrant flowers produced in small clusters along last year's shoots. New growths can be susceptible to spring frosts. They thrive on all soils in full sun or very light shade. After flowering, the older shoots should be removed to encourage strong long new growths.

D. × elegantissima 'Rosealind'   Forms rounded bush, 3–4 ft (1–1.2 m) high and wide, with deep carmine flowers. *D. × rosea* 'Carminea', flowers rose-carmine in bud, fading on opening (see p.210).

D. 'Magicien'   Grows to 6½ by 4 ft (2 × 1.2 m). Flowers large, pink tinted with a white edge and purple-streaked reverse. 'Mont Rose', rose-pink flowers with a deeper tint. *D. scabra* 'Candidissima', pure white, double flowers.

Elaeagnus umbellata   Rich fragrance of the flowers is detectable from several yards away, although these are small, creamy white and actually rather lost against the silvery foliage. Mature leaves bright green above and silvery beneath. Fruits orange-red. Forms bush, 10 ft (3 m) high and across, but can be restrained by pruning. Sun or light shade.

Genista lydia   A broom which has very wiry, green, pendulous shoots and fleeting leaves. Small arching plant, 2 by 2½ ft (0.6 × 0.8 m), with bright yellow flowers. Very effective at the front of a border or at the top of a sunny wall. Prune only into green shoots. Sun. Any well-drained soil.

Hebe   Evergreens with dense opposite leaves. Not particular about soil, apart from needing good drainage, but often damaged by severe winters and tend to be short-lived. They do not like pruning and should only ever be cut back to wood which is still green and leafy.

H. hulkeana (New Zealand lilac)   Sprawling shrub, 3 by 6½ ft (1 × 2 m) and the most spectacular hebe for flowers. These are small, delicate lavender or lilac, carried in enormous panicles at the ends of the shoots. Succeeds best against a sunny wall with good drainage.

H. pinguifolia 'Pagei'   Low shrub, 1 by 3 ft (0.3 × 1 m), with abundant white flowers. Perhaps its chief merit is the persistent, glaucous blue foliage.

Kalmia latifolia (calico bush)   Rhododendron-like plant with glossy evergreen foliage and beautiful saucer-shaped flowers, pink or red depending on cultivar.

Above: 'Kiwi' and other forms of *Leptospermum scoparium* thrive in the warmer southwestern counties of Britain
Below: *Poncirus trifoliata*, known as the Japanese bitter orange, is hardy and easily grown

Above: The free-flowering 'Goldfinger', one of many hybrids of the versatile *Potentilla fruticosa*

Below: *Rhododendron yakushimanum* is one of the most desirable small species and will even withstand full sun

Moist acid soil with light shade. Slow-growing, 5 ft (1.5 m) high and broad (see p.208).

Kolkwitzia amabilis 'Pink Beauty' Broad rounded bush, approximately 6 ft (1.8 m) tall and wide. Flowers on spur shoots produced off last season's growths, each spur terminating in a cluster of bell-shaped pink blooms. The fruits are curiously bristly and the leaves turn pinkish in autumn. Prune after flowering to replace three-year-old shoots. Sun or light shade.

Leptospermum scoparium (manuka, tea tree) Very twiggy dense evergreen, 8 ft (2.5 m) high, although with time in mild areas will make a small tree. Grown for beauty of the white flowers, which smother the foliage. Small evergreen leaves are aromatic if bruised. Not long-lived in most gardens, needing either the shelter of other plants or a position at the base of a wall. Full sun. 'Kiwi', low-growing with dark red, single flowers and bronze-tinted leaves (see p.219). 'Nicholsii', bright crimson flowers and bronze-red leaves. 'Red Damask', flowers fully double, deep cherry-red. 'Snow Flurry', white double flowers.

Lonicera syringantha Elegant plant, 3–5 by 5 ft (1–1.5 × 1.5 m), with fragrant, soft lilac flowers. Sun or light shade. Like other shrubby honeysuckles, deserves to be more widely used in gardens.

Poncirus trifoliata Unusual slow-growing relative of the lemon, 6½ ft (2 m) high and across, with strongly spined, matt green shoots. Sweetly scented 2 in. (5 cm) white flowers produced before the trifoliate leaves from axils of the spines, followed by bitter oranges with thick wrinkled skin. Sun or light shade (see p.219).

Potentilla (cinquefoil) Small shrubs valued for the length of the flowering season, from late May into early autumn. They grow on a wide range of soils in full sun or light shade and make excellent hedges. Young plants can be cut back to ground level, in older plants only old shoots should be removed. They have a peeling bark.

P. davurica 'Manchu' White flowers and grey-green foliage. Forms a spreading dwarf bush, 2–3 by 3 ft (0.6–1 × 1 m).

P. fruticosa Domed spreading plant, usually 3–4 by 3–5 ft (1–1.2 × 1–1.5 m), but only 2 ft (0.6 m) high in 'Sunset'. Most selections have yellow flowers, such as 'Elizabeth', 'Goldfinger' and 'Katherine Dykes'. 'Sunset', flowers deep orange to brick red. 'Vilmoriniana', cream-coloured flowers. 'Red Ace', glowing red flowers, better in light shade.

Rhododendron yakushimanum Slowly forms a rounded evergreen bush, 3 by 5 ft (1 × 1.5 m), with glossy, dark green leaves felted and richly coloured beneath. In bud the flowers are deep pink, paling as they open to white, carried in rounded trusses (see also Rhododendron, p.213, for cultivation requirements).

Japanese azaleas Low-growing evergreen bushes, 3–5 by 5 ft (1–1.5 × 1.5 m), which give an overwhelming display when covered in the large flowers. They need light shade and can be trimmed after flowering to prevent them getting too large and leggy. Selections available include 'Hinodegiri', crimson-scarlet flowers with deep coloured throat; 'Hinomayo', phlox-pink; and 'Palestrina', white.

Deciduous azaleas Bushes 3–6½ by 5 ft (1–2 × 1.5 m), with good autumn foliage colours. Sun or light shade. Among the many hybrids are 'Gibraltar', flowers dark red in bud opening to flame-orange with a yellow flash; 'Homebush', rose-madder, semi-double, in very neat rounded trusses; 'Klondyke', orange-gold with a red tint; 'Koster's Brilliant Red', glowing orange-red; and 'Persil', white with orange flare.

Rosa (rose) Hybrid tea and floribunda roses are grown in nearly all gardens, but are in many ways less suitable as shrubs for general use – and more demanding of attention – than the species, climbers and old-fashioned varieties. These thrive on all soils, although doing less well on shallow soils over chalk, require very little pruning, except to remove old wood, and will grow in sun or light shade.

R. elegantula (R. farreri) **'Persetosa'** Rounded bush up to 6½ ft (2 m) high, with masses of small pink flowers displayed against dainty fern-like foliage and small, bright red hips.

R. pimpinellifolia (Scotch or burnet rose) Low, suckering, very thorny shrub, up to 3 ft (1 m) high, especially suited to dry soils. Pale pink or creamy white flowers succeeded by black fruits.

R. xanthina 'Canary Bird' Large, fragrant, single, deep canary-yellow flowers carried for a month and repeated later in the year. Fresh green fern-like foliage. Makes a bush 6½ ft (2 m) high and across, almost devoid of prickles. R. 'Helen Knight', similar, with clear yellow saucer-shaped flowers and smaller leaves; grows 3–5 ft (1–1.5 m) tall.

Rosmarinus officinalis (rosemary) Erect dense evergreen, 6½ by 5 ft (2 × 1.5 m). Narrow leaves grey-green or green and white-felted beneath. Sun. Any well-drained soil. 'Severn Sea', brilliant blue flowers, arching habit, 2 ft (0.6 m) tall.

Rubus 'Beneden' Large white dog-rose flowers, faintly scented, on the previous season's shoots and fresh green, palmately lobed leaves. Makes a bush 6½ ft (2 m) tall and broad. Prune by removing old wood after flowering. Sun to moderate shade.

Syringa (lilac) Cultivars of common lilac generally offered will grow into small trees, but the following are very attractive and unusual shrubs. They need well-drained soil, full sun or very light shade and protection from frost. Do not prune except to control size.

S. microphylla 'Superba' Small oval leaves and a mass of fragrant, rosy pink flowers, mainly in May but intermittently until October. Grows to 5 by 3 ft (1.5 × 1 m) (see p.198).

S. × persica Spreading rounded bush, 3–5 by 5–6½ ft (1–1.5 × 1.5–2 m), with lilac-coloured flowers, white in 'Alba'.

Viburnum plicatum 'Mariesii' Spreading bush, 3–5 by 5–6½ ft (1–1.5 × 1.5–2 m), with abundant white flowers borne above the tiered foliage and leaves changing dull crimson in autumn. 'Pink Beauty', narrower in habit with flowers turning pink as they age. 'Rowallane', similar to 'Mariesii', but more reliable in production of bright red fruits. Sun or light shade.

Wisteria sinensis Climber capable of reaching 70 ft (20 m) up an oak tree, but can be grown against a house wall or trained as free-standing shrub. Large trusses of fragrant, deep lilac flowers hang below branches, with attractive pinnate leaves. Prune by shortening long whippy shoots to 6 in. (15 cm) in August and to two to three buds after leaf fall. Full sun. W. floribunda 'Macrobotrys', racemes of flowers up to 3 ft (1 m) long.

MIDSUMMER FLOWERS – JUNE TO JULY

Abutilon × suntense Erect shrub, 6½–10 by 3–5 ft (2–3 × 1–1.5 m), needing a sheltered site or warm sunny wall. Palmate, felted, grey leaves and masses of saucer-shaped flowers carried over a long period from midsummer on. Sun or light shade. Any well-drained soil. 'Jermyns', clear dark mauve flowers. 'Geoffrey Gorer' and 'White Charm', white.

Buddleia davidii (butterfly bush) Can be grown as a small tree, but is usually coppiced (i.e. pruned to ground level or a short stem) in March to produce long flowering shoots from July onwards; treated like this, it reaches 5–10 by 5–6½ ft (1.5–3 × 1.5–2 m). Flowers richly scented and attractive to butterflies. Seedlings have inferior flowers, and named clones should always be used, such as 'Black Knight', with dark violet flowers, and 'Royal Red', red-purple. Pruning is not essential and unpruned plants will flower earlier, with more numerous, smaller trusses. Sun or light shade.

Calycanthus floridus Grows to 5 ft (1.5 m) high and wide, with reddish purple flowers, very strongly scented. The leaves, wood and bark all have a camphor-like fragrance if bruised. Sun to moderate shade.

Above: 'Canary Bird', the commonest representative in gardens of *Rosa xanthina*, is a fine arching shrub

Below: *Viburnum plicatum* 'Rowallane' is more moderate in growth than 'Mariesii'

Above: The rock roses, including *Cistus* × *lusitanicus* 'Decumbens', are tolerant of wind and coastal exposure and happy on chalk soils

Below: The pink broom of New Zealand, *Notospartium carmichaeliae*, should survive most winters once established

Cistus (rock or sun rose) Evergreen shrubs needing full sun and tolerating dry sites. They cannot be pruned effectively and are short-lived, although very attractive. Large showy flowers open for a single morning, dropping the petals in the afternoon, but are produced in such numbers as to prolong the display. Any well-drained soil.

C. laurifolius White flowers with yellow boss of stamens carried from June to August. Upright shrub, 6½ by 3–5 ft (1 × 1–1.5 m), with a peeling purple bark. The hardiest species.

C. × lusitanicus 'Decumbens' Spreading bush, 3 by 5 ft (1 × 1.5 m). Flowers have white petals with basal crimson-purple blotch and central boss of golden stamens, borne from June into September.

C. × purpureus Grey-green aromatic leaves and large flowers with reddish pink petals and chocolate blotch. Not reliably hardy. Grows to 4 by 5 ft (1.2 × 1.5 m).

C. 'Silver Pink' Hardy form having long clusters of silver-pink flowers with golden stamens. Prefers richer soil than most rock roses. Grows to 2¼ by 3–5 ft (0.7 × 1–1.5 m).

Escallonia Evergreen shrubs which tolerate a wide range of soils and also maritime conditions. Many are not fully hardy. Flowering starts in June on last year's shoots and continues into autumn on current season's growths. They may be pruned to shape immediately after flowering, especially if grown against a wall or as a hedge. Unpruned, they grow 5–8 ft (1.5–2.5 m) tall. Sun to light shade.

E. 'Apple Blossom' Pink and white flowers. 'Donard Star', rose-pink flowers and larger, dark glossy green leaves. 'Edinensis', rose-pink flowers.

E. rubra 'Woodside' Smaller-growing, with a rounded habit, up to 2 ft (0.6 m) high, and rosy crimson flowers. Inclined to throw up vigorous shoots which should be removed.

Hebe armstrongii Yellow ochre-coloured whip-like shoots covered with small scale-leaves, forming a bush 1½ by 2 ft (0.5 × 0.6 m). Flowers in short white spikes (see also *Hebe*, p.218, for cultivation requirements).

H. 'Carl Teschner' Low mound, 8 in. by 2½ ft (0.2 × 0.8 m). Small leaves and violet flowers with a white throat.

Ligustrum sinense 'Pendulum' Rounded bush 5–6½ by 8 ft (1.5–2 × 2.5 m), with hanging shoots and large numbers of very fragrant, white flowers. Sun to light shade.

Lonicera caprifolium An early-flowering honeysuckle with very fragrant, creamy white flowers. Climber, growing 13–16½ ft (4–5 m) high. Sun or light shade.

Notospartium carmichaeliae Graceful arching habit, 4 ft (1.2 m) high, with lilac-pink pea flowers on leafless green shoots. May be killed by severe winters when young and needs well-drained soil. Full sun.

Olearia nummulariifolia Rounded evergreen bush, 5 ft (1.5m) high, with small thickly set, yellow-green leaves and scented white daisy flowers. Sun.

Rhododendron viscosum (swamp honeysuckle) Deciduous azalea producing very strongly scented, white or pink flowers which are sticky outside. Grows to 6½ ft (2 m) tall. Sun or light shade. Acid soils only, tolerating wet ones.

Rosa 'Buff Beauty' Hybrid musk rose with double apricot-yellow tea-scented flowers borne in successive flushes. Grows to 6 ft (1.8 m) tall and has coppery brown young foliage. May be hard pruned in spring or allowed to grow over large shrubs or small trees (see also *Rosa*, p.221, for cultivation requirements).

R. 'Maiden's Blush' Old-fashioned variety making a bush 4 ft (1.2 m) high, with healthy grey-green foliage. Flowers blush-pink, sweetly scented and very double. Prune out old shoots only.

R. rugosa 'Fru Dagmar Hastrup' Low-growing form of Ramanas rose, attaining 3 ft (1 m) high. Single flowers vivid pink in bud, opening to rose-pink, followed by large crimson edible hips rich in vitamin C. It suckers and is excellent for hedging.

Can be cut down to ground level in spring and will still flower by midsummer. Especially useful on sandy soils.

R. virginiana Small suckering rose 2 ft (0.6 m) high. Bright pink flowers, giving way to small rounded red fruits, and leaves also turning a fine colour in autumn. Good on sandy soils.

Salvia officinalis 'Icterina' Form of common sage with fragrant leaves variegated with yellow and light green. Evergreen, growing to 2 by 2½ ft (0.6 × 0.8 m). Sun. Any, especially light, soils.

Santolina chamaecyparissus (cotton lavender)   Low bush, 1¼ by 2½ ft (0.4 × 0.8 m), with silvery evergreen foliage deeply cut as in filigree lace. Flowers are attractive yellow buttons. Flowering plants, however, lose their shapeliness; for maximum foliage effect, hard prune in April to promote vigorous leaf growth. Sun. Any, especially light, soils.

LATE SUMMER FLOWERS – JULY TO SEPTEMBER

Abelia × grandiflora   Graceful shrub, 5 ft (1.5 m) high and wide, with bright green, evergreen foliage. Softly fragrant flowers carried on current season's growth from July into October, white tinged pale pink. Full sun. In coldest districts, place against a wall. 'Francis Mason', golden yellow foliage.

Aesculus parviflora   Shrubby suckering horse chestnut, forming rounded clump 5–6½ by 10–13 ft (1.5–2 × 3–4 m). Leaves have five palmate leaflets, turning good colours in autumn. Flowers in glowing white candles 8–12 in. (20–30 cm) long. Sun to light shade.

Callistemon citrinus 'Splendens'   Evergreen shrub, 3–5 by 5 ft (1–1.5 × 1.5 m), suitable for mild areas or set against a wall in full sun. Brilliant scarlet bottle-brush flowers. The leaves are lemon-scented when crushed. Not for chalk soils.

Calluna vulgaris (heather, ling)   Native evergreen shrub, low and spreading, up to 1½ ft (0.5 m) high. Available in numerous forms, useful for both flowers and foliage. Prune by clipping after flowering. Sun or light shade. Acid soils only. 'Blazeaway', lilac-mauve flowers and green foliage which turns red in winter. 'Darkness', deep rose-purple flowers. 'Peter Sparkes', double pink. Gold foliage forms include 'Beoley Gold', 'Gold Haze' and 'Serlei', all with white flowers.

Caryopteris × clandonensis 'Heavenly Blue'   Low-growing, up to 2½ ft (0.8 m) tall, with deep blue flowers. Prune to ground level in spring. Sun. Any well-drained soil.

Ceratostigma willmottianum   Grows 2½ by 2 ft (0.8 × 0.6 m), with the leaves turning red in autumn. Bright blue flowers from July into October. Prune to ground level in spring (if winter cold has not done so!). Full sun. Dry well-drained soils.

Clematis vernayi (*C. orientalis*) (orange peel clematis)   Climber flowering on current year's shoots. The yellow flowers have thick fleshy "petals", likened to orange peel, and are succeeded by silky seedheads. The greyish leaves are deeply cut. If left unpruned it will grow to 20 ft (6 m), if cut to ground in late winter it will reach 10–13 ft (3–4 m). Sun to light shade.

Clerodendron trichotomum var. fargesii   Large rounded shrub, 8 ft (2.5 m) high. Fragrant white star-shaped flowers, followed by porcelain-blue berries set off by persistent crimson sepals. Sun or light shade.

Clethra alnifolia (sweet pepper bush)   Reaches 5 by 3 ft (1.5 × 1 m). Flowers are strongly fragrant in erect, creamy white, 6 in. (15 cm) sprays. Prune by removing older stems in winter. Light to moderate shade. Moist lime-free soils. 'Rosea', pink in bud.

Cotinus coggygria (smoke bush)   With time, forms a sprawling bush 10–13 ft (3–4 m) tall, with rounded green leaves turning brilliant red in autumn. Flowers in large clusters, attractive for their many slender silky-haired stalks which start pale

Above: The decorative hips of *Rosa rugosa* 'Fru Dagmar Hastrup' (left); *Ceratostigma willmottianum* (right) contributes a welcome blue in late summer

Below: *Callistemon citrinus* 'Splendens' (left), an eye-catching feature; the conspicuous seedheads of *Clematis vernayi* (right)

The smoke bush, *Cotinus coggygria*, makes the most impressive display
of flowers if the soil is not too rich

flesh colour and become smoky grey by autumn. Prune to restrict size. Sun or light
shade. 'Royal Purple', purple foliage.

Daboecia cantabrica   Evergreen heath, up to 1½ ft (0.5 m) tall. The flowers are
pendent bells in erect terminal racemes, white in 'Alba', deep purple in 'Atropurpurea'. Prune by clipping to remove spent flower heads. Sun or light shade.
Acid soils only.

Desfontainea spinosa   Evergreen, 5 by 4 ft (1.5 × 1.2 m), with spiny shiny holly-like
leaves. Large tubular flowers, with a crimson scarlet tube and yellow lobes. Needs
a sheltered position. Light shade. Moist lime-free soil (see p.200).

Deutzia monbeigii   Grows to 4 ft (1.2 m) tall and across. The small leaves are white
beneath, giving a grey tone to the plant. Carries clusters of glistening white star-
shaped flowers (see also *Deutzia*, p.218, for cultivation requirements).

Erica (heather)   *E. cinerea*, *E. tetralix* and *E. vagans* and their forms are spreading
evergreen shrubs with bell-shaped white, pink or crimson flowers. Like *Calluna*
and *Daboecia*, they should be planted in groups, at about 5 to 10 plants per square
yard. They will grow 1 ft (0.3 m) tall, but are best clipped after flowering to prevent
them getting leggy. Sun. Acid soils only.

Fremontodendron 'California Glory'   Only hardy for a few average winters with
the protection of a warm sunny wall, but well worth trying. Evergreen erect shrub,
10–13 by 5–6½ ft (3–4 × 1.5–2 m), with large, bright lemon yellow flowers over an ex-
tended period. South-facing aspect. Any well-drained soil.

Hebe 'Autumn Glory'   Succession of intense violet-blue flowers until stopped by
frost. Leaves glossy green with purple tinge. Makes an erect spreading bush, 2 by
2½ ft (0.6 × 0.8 m) (see p.230 and also *Hebe*, p.218, for cultivation requirements).

H. × franciscana 'Blue Gem'   Hardier than most hebes, forming a compact
dome-shaped bush, 2 ft (0.6 m) high and broad, with fresh green leaves and bright
blue flowers.

H. 'Great Orme' Displays bright pink flowers against large spear-shaped leaves. Compact bush, 2½ ft (0.8 m) tall and across.

Hibiscus syriacus Grows 10–13 ft (3–4 m) high, but easily restricted by pruning in late winter. Produces hollyhock-like flowers on current season's shoots. Full sun. Any well-drained soil. 'Blue Bird', bright blue flowers up to 3 in. (8 cm) in diameter. 'Diana', white (see p.208). 'Woodbridge', rich pink.

Hydrangea arborescens 'Annabelle' Low-growing shrub, 3 by 5 ft (1 × 1.5 m), which carries very large heads of glistening white flowers. Needs moist soil, but will take full sun to moderate shade. Prune by removing spent flowers.

H. paniculata Large shrub or can be grown into a small tree, 13 ft (4 m) or more high. May be hard pruned in late winter to produce larger panicles of flowers, which are in triangular heads and creamy white, ageing to pinkish. 'Praecox', first to flower in July, followed by 'Grandiflora', then 'Tardiva' in September and early October.

H. serrata 'Preziosa' Small-flowered but very hardy hortensia hydrangea, growing to 4 by 3 ft (1.2 × 1 m). Flowers salmon-pink, later warm red, and foliage attractively tinged purple when young. Sun or light shade (see p.230).

Hypericum forrestii Upright evergreen or semi-evergreen bush, 3–5 by 3 ft (1–1.5 × 1 m). Can be hard pruned in spring and will produce large golden yellow flowers, followed by bronzy red young fruits. Sun. Any well-drained soil. H. 'Hidcote', more compact rounded bush with a longer flowering season until cut by autumn frosts, but rarely fruits.

Indigofera heterantha Develops luxuriant feathery or pinnate foliage on long wand-like shoots, with rosy purple pea flowers. Cut back to ground level in spring, when it will reach 5 ft (1.5 m) high and wide. Sun. Any well-drained soil (see p.231).

Lavandula angustifolia (lavender) Dwarf evergreen shrub, 2½ ft (0.8 m) tall and across, with silvery grey foliage and fragrant blue flowers. Sun. Any well-drained soil. 'Hidcote', smaller form with purple flowers.

Lonicera × brownii 'Dropmore Scarlet' Vigorous climbing honeysuckle, 10–13 ft (3–4 m) high, with clusters of bright scarlet, tubular flowers from July into October. Sun or light shade.

Olearia × haastii Rounded shrub, 4 ft (1.2 m) high and wide, with small evergreen leaves, grey beneath. Fragrant white flowers in large daisy-like heads. No pruning necessary except for hedges. Sun.

O. macrodonta (New Zealand holly) Large sage-green spined leaves, richly silvered beneath. Evergreen, 6½ ft (2 m) tall and broad, with fragrant white flowers in large clusters. Less reliably hardy, but excellent for coastal situations. Sun or light shade.

Senecio compactus Crinkled leaves felted pure white beneath and yellow daisy flowers. Compact evergreen shrub, 3 by 5–6½ ft (1 × 1.5–2 m). Cut back in spring to two to three buds to control size. Sun or light shade. Any well-drained soil. S. 'Sunshine', better flowers but grey-green leaves.

S. scandens Strong-growing climber up to 10–13 ft (3–4 m), with masses of yellow daisy flowers. Slightly tender and needs a sheltered site in sun. It can be cut back hard in spring, if not killed back by winter cold.

Solanum crispum 'Glasnevin' Climber with potato flowers of rich purple-blue with yellow centres over a long period. Can be pruned back in spring and will reach 13–20 ft (4–6 m). Requires a sheltered position in full sun (see p.231).

Spiraea japonica Grows into a rounded shrub, 5 by 6½ ft (1.5 × 2 m), with rose-pink flowers. Prune by removing surplus old shoots in spring and shortening those remaining. Sun or light shade. 'Gold Flame' (S. × bumalda 'Gold Flame'), new foliage golden yellow with bronzy red tips, becoming greener with age; needs moist soil (see p.195). 'Little Princess', mound-forming, 3 × 6½ ft (1 × 2 m), with rose-crimson flowers. 'Shirobani', flowers white, becoming deep pink.

229

Above: *Hebe* 'Autumn Glory' needs a well-drained soil and flowers almost continuously from midsummer on

Below: Like all hydrangeas, *H. serrata* 'Preziosa' prefers a moist soil doing well in sun or semi-shade

Above: *Indigofera heterantha* remains in flower throughout summer and autumn

Below: *Solanum crispum* 'Glasnevin', a vigorous semi-evergreen climber which flourishes in chalky soils

AUTUMN EFFECT

The following shrubs produce decorative fruits, which often persist over winter. Several other shrubs are valuable for autumn flowers (see pp.226–229) or foliage (see pp.237–240).

Callicarpa bodinieri 'Profusion'   Erect shrub, 6½ by 4 ft (2 x 1.2 m). Purple-blue fruits in clusters along the previous year's shoots make a striking display after leaf fall and remain into winter. They are preceded by mauve-pink flowers in July and August. Prune to remove old stems. Sun or light shade.

Cotoneaster   Versatile shrubs for sun or light shade, tolerating wide range of soils.

C. bullatus   Grows to 8 by 6½ ft (2.5 x 2 m) and gives brilliant fiery autumn colours from the large corrugated leaves. Berries bright red.

C. conspicuus   Spreading mound, 3 by 5–6½ ft (1 x 1.5–2 m), with small evergreen foliage and showy white flowers in early summer. The abundant, bright red, juicy berries, which may persist until Easter, are the best feature.

C. franchetti   Oval orange-scarlet berries lasting until Christmas or beyond. Small evergreen sage-green leaves and a graceful arching habit, 6½ ft (2 m) high and across.

C. horizontalis   Spreading, with herring-bone pattern branches. Mainly grown as a wall shrub, reaching 6½–13 ft (2–4 m) or more; otherwise, forms a mound, 1½–3 by 5 ft (0.5–1 x 1.5 m). Berries scarlet and small glossy leaves which turn orange before falling.

C. lacteus   Leathery oval evergreen leaves provide a foil for the milky white flowers in June and later for the long-lasting red fruits. Makes a shrub 10 ft (3 m) high and wide. Prune to control size.

Euonymus alatus 'Compacta'   Mound-shaped bush, 2½ by 4 ft (0.8 x 1.2 m). The foliage turns brilliant red in autumn and the twigs have curious corky wings. Sun or light shade.

Ilex cornuta   Evergreen holly, 3 by 5 ft (1 x 1.5 m), with strangely shaped, glossy green leaves – rectangular, having scalloped margins and five spines. Berries red. Sun or light shade.

I. crenata 'Mariesii'   Erect evergreen, 4 by 2½ ft (1.2 x 0.8 m), with black berries. Sun or light shade.

Pernettya mucronata   Suckering evergreen shrub, 1½–3 by 3 ft (0.5–1 x 1 m) or more. Small white bell-shaped flowers followed, on female plants, by large white or coloured berries which remain over winter. One male plant must be planted to every 3 to 5 female ones. They associate well with heathers. Sun or light shade. Acid soils only. 'Bell's Seedling', red berries. 'Cherry Ripe', bright cherry-red ones (see p.196). 'Mother of Pearl', light pink berries. 'White Pearl', glistening white.

Ruscus aculeatus (butcher's broom)   Evergreen member of the lily family. The "leaves" are modified shoots and on female plants carry flowers in the centre, giving large red berries in autumn. Suckering shrub, 1½ by 3 ft (0.5 x 1 m). Light to deep shade.

Sorbus reducta   Dwarf suckering rowan, 3 by 1½–5 ft (1 x 0.5–1.5 m). Fruits pinky white and pinnate leaves turn bronze and purple before falling in autumn. Sun to light shade. Neutral to acid soils.

Symphoricarpos   Useful shrubs with colourful berries which tolerate quite shady positions.

S. x chenaultii 'Hancock'   Dwarf suckering plant, 2 by 8 ft (0.6 x 2.5 m), with pinkish purple berries. 'Magic Berry', abundant lilac-carmine berries, 4 ft (1.2 m) high and across. 'Mother of Pearl', arching habit, 5 ft (1.5 m) tall and wide, with white berries tinted pink.

Above: *Callicarpa bodinieri* 'Profusion' (left) does not need to be grown in groups to produce its unusual fruits; *Cotoneaster bullatus* (right), with its glistening red berries and attractive foliage, is an excellent species

Below: The bold evergreen foliage of *Viburnum davidii* is enhanced by the blue berries

Viburnum davidii Dense low mound, 2¼ by 5 ft (0.8 × 1.5 m), although old plants may grow 5 ft (1.5 m) tall. Deep green, evergreen leaves have three prominent veins. Turquoise-blue berries which persist over winter are the main attraction. Plant two or more for pollination of female plants. Sun to moderate shade (see p.233).

WINTER EFFECT – DECEMBER TO FEBRUARY/MARCH

Chimonanthus praecox (winter sweet) Bushy shrub up to 8 ft (2.5 m) tall, often grown against a wall. Ivory to yellow flowers very pleasantly scented and borne over a long period. The leaves also have a spicy fragrance. Sun to light shade.

Cornus alba (dogwood) Grown mainly for pronounced red colour of the one-year-old shoots. Best if hard pruned to ground annually at end of March, then growing to 3–4 ft (1–1.2 m) high and wide. Sun to light shade. Any soil, especially wet ones. 'Elegantissima', green and silver variegated foliage. 'Spaethii', golden variegated foliage; both also have good barks.
C. stolonifera 'Flaviramea' Lemon-yellow winter shoots, going well with the red-stemmed dogwoods (see p.196).

Corylus avellana 'Contorta' (corkscrew hazel) Twisted and curled branches give an interesting winter silhouette, with yellow hanging catkins in February. Grows 6½–10 by 6½ ft (2–3 × 2 m). Tolerates full sun to moderate shade.

Daphne bholua Deciduous or semi-evergreen erect shrub, 5 by 3 ft (1.5 × 1 m), with a long succession of rose-purple richly scented flowers. Sun or light shade. 'Gurkha' and 'Jacqueline Postill', named forms.

Erica herbacea (*E. carnea*) (heath) Flowers from January to March and, unlike other heaths, will grow on all soils, including those on chalk. Spreading low shrub, 4–12 in. (10–30 cm) tall. Clip after flowering. Sun or light shade. Good forms are 'King George', early, from November, flowers carmine; 'Springwood White', best white; 'Springwood Pink', rose-pink; and 'Vivellii', deep red with dark bronze winter foliage. On acid soils, coloured foliage forms of *Calluna vulgaris* (see p.226) can also be used.

Garrya elliptica 'James Roof' Grown for the male catkins up to 14 in. (35 cm) long. Evergreen rounded shrub 10 ft high, but often grown against a wall, particularly in cold districts. Prune to control size after flowering. Sun or light shade. Good for north and east aspects.

Lonicera fragrantissima Shrubby honeysuckle growing 6 ft (1.8 m) tall and across, with cream-coloured strongly fragrant flowers. Red berries may follow in May. Sun to light shade.

Mahonia × media Bold-foliaged evergreen capable of forming a small tree after 15 to 20 years, but after ten years only 6½ by 5 ft (2 × 1.5 m). Leaves set in rosettes at tips of shoots, in which are carried fragrant yellow flowers from October until after Christmas. Sun to moderate shade. Good named forms include 'Lionel Fortescue', 'Buckland' and 'Charity'.

Rhododendron mucronulatum Erect semi-evergreen shrub, 5 ft (1.5 m) high, with delightful, bright rose-purple flowers. Needs siting where it will not be caught by morning sun, as the blossoms can be damaged by frost. Light to moderate shade. Acid soils only.

Sarcococca humilis Dense evergreen suckering shrub, 1½ by 3 ft (0.5 × 1 m). White flowers, richly scented, lead to black berries. Sun to moderate shade.
S. ruscifolia Erect evergreen bush, 4 by 3 ft (1.2 × 1 m), with crimson berries.

Viburnum farreri Starts flowering as the leaves drop in autumn and continues until February, depending upon weather. Flowers fragrant, pale pink in bud opening to white. Less showy in flower than V. × *bodnantense* forms, such as 'Deben' and 'Dawn', but superior for the erect habit with spreading branches, 6½ by 4 ft (2 × 1.2 m), and for the neat foliage with bronze new growths.

Above: *Cornus alba* 'Elegantissima' (left), a variegated form of the dogwood which is less rampant than the species itself; the curious corkscrew hazel, *Corylus avellana* 'Contorta' (right), was originally discovered in a Gloucestershire hedgerow

Below: *Viburnum farreri*, still better known as *V. fragrans*, is a favourite shrub for the winter garden

Above: The climbing *Actinidia kolomikta* should be pruned in winter

Below: *Berberis thunbergii* 'Atropurpurea Nana', a useful dwarf bush for massing or as a low hedge

YEAR-ROUND INTEREST

Shrubs grown primarily for the beauty of their foliage can provide colour, shape and texture throughout the year and several are also attractive in flower. Similarly, many of the flowering shrubs already described are useful for their decorative foliage.

Dwarf conifers also supply permanent interest and add an element of scale, grandeur or variety to a garden setting, particularly when associated with heathers and other rather flat plants or in a rock garden. They require no pruning and are suitable for full sun to light shade and any soil. (See also the Wisley Handbooks, *Foliage Plants* and *Dwarf and Slow-growing Conifers*.)

Abies nordmanniana 'Golden Spreader' Upright, normally flat-topped fir up to 3 ft (1 m) high; with dense, bright golden yellow foliage. Better sited in light shade, as in full sun the colour may be bleached; in deep shade it becomes greener.
A. lasiocarpa 'Compacta' Bright blue-grey foliage on a neat conical plant. Grows 3–4 ft (1–1.2 m) tall in ten years, eventually reaching 10–13 ft (3–4 m).
Acer palmatum 'Bloodgood' A superior selection of Japanese maple with rich red-purple leaves which retain colour well throughout summer, turning bright red before falling. Makes an upright rounded bush, 8 ft (2.5 m) high. Sun or light shade. Any soil, better in acid ones.
A. palmatum 'Dissectum' Bright green, deeply divided foliage. Forms a shapely rounded bush, 2 by 3 ft (0.6 × 1 m), and is well placed drooping over a low wall. The autumn colour is bronzy yellow (see p.187).
Actinidia kolomikta Climber up to 10–13 ft (3–4 m), with large leaves which become white flushed with pink on top half. The colour is stronger in full sun, but will take light shade. White flowers in June are slightly fragrant. Prune to restrain.
Artemisia 'Powis Castle' Dome, 2–3 by 3–4 ft (0.6–1 × 1–1.2 m), with silvery leaves which are deeply cut like lace filigree. Prune by cutting back to near ground level in spring. Sun.
Arundinaria murieliae Strong-growing but non-invasive bamboo. Forms rounded mop-head of rich green, nearly evergreen leaves on cluster of green or yellow stems, up to 10–13 ft (3–4 m) tall and across. Prune by removing old stems. Light to deep shade. Any moist soil.
Berberis thunbergii Barberry growing to 5 by 4 ft (1.5 × 1.2 m), with sealing wax red berries and brilliant autumn colours. Sun or light shade. 'Aurea', leaves yellow, becoming light green. 'Atropurpurea Nana', dwarf form 2 ft (0.6 m) high, with purple foliage. 'Red Chief', good wine red foliage on upright arching bush, 6 by 5 ft (1.8 × 1.5 m). 'Rose Glow', young leaves purple with silver-pink and rose mottling, becoming plain purple as they age (see also p.193).
Cedrus deodora 'Golden Horizon' Spreading form of deodar cedar with golden foliage, 3 by 6½–10 ft (1 × 2–3 m). The foliage becomes more bluish green in shade.
Chamaecyparis pisifera 'Filifera Aurea' Long whip-like golden-yellow shoots pendulous at tips, forming an attractive mound, 3 by 4 ft (1 × 1.2 m), slowly increasing to 10–13 ft (3–4 m) tall.
Elaeagnus × ebbingei Evergreen bush, 10 ft (3 m) high and across, with leaves silvery beneath. Unusual for carrying the very fragrant pale flowers in October. Sun or light shade. Any except shallow chalk soil. 'Gilt Edge', leaves margined with gold. 'Limelight', leaves with large deep yellow centre. Remove all shoots which have reverted to pure green as soon as possible.
Euonymus fortunei Evergreen climber which has given rise to several small low-growing forms, 1 by 2–3 ft (0.3 × 0.6–1 m), making good groundcover with their

colourful foliage. Sun to deep shade. 'Emerald Gaiety', green leaves with silver variegation. 'Emerald 'n' Gold', gold-variegated foliage turning pinkish in winter. 'Silver Queen', creamy white-variegated.

Fothergilla major　Rounded bush to 3–5 ft (1–1.5 m) high and wide, with two conspicuous seasons of display – red, orange or yellow foliage in autumn and fragrant white bottle-brush flowers before the leaves in April and May. Light shade. Acid soils only (see also p.250).

Hedera algeriensis (*H. canariensis*) **Gloire de Marengo'**　Large variegated leaves deep green in the centre, creamy white on the margins and silvery-grey in patches. A useful evergreen self-clinging climber for covering walls, sheds and trees. Sun or light shade (see p.187).

H. helix 'Conglomerata Erecta'　Non-clinging form of common ivy, with stiffly erect-growing shoots to 3 ft (1 m) high, making a low hummock, and evergreen leaves arranged in two rows. 'Congesta' is similar. 'Buttercup', vigorous climber with leaves of rich yellow, paling with age (see p.240). Sun to deep shade.

Juniperus horizontalis　Ground-hugging juniper growing no higher than 4–6 in. (10–15 cm), but covering 6½–10 ft (2–3 m) and particularly useful as a foil for dwarf bulbs or as low groundcover. 'Douglasii', foliage bright glaucous green in summer, developing a purplish tinge over winter. 'Wiltonii', glaucous blue leaves.

J. squamata 'Blue Carpet'　Foliage of intense steely blue, growing 1 by 3–6½ ft (0.3 × 1–2 m). 'Blue Star', similar in colour, remaining low and compact, 1 by 1½ ft (0.3 × 0.5 m).

Lonicera nitida 'Baggesen's Gold'　Shrubby evergreen honeysuckle with bright golden yellow leaves, becoming yellowish green in autumn, and dense arching habit, to 4 by 3 ft (1.2 × 1 m). Sun or light shade.

Nandina domestica (heavenly bamboo)　Unbranched erect stems 4 ft (1.2 m) tall, bearing rosettes of compound evergreen foliage. The leaves are crimson and scarlet when young and also in autumn. Small white flowers in large terminal clusters in June and July, followed by red berries. Sun to moderate shade.

Parthenocissus henryana　Vigorous climber up to 16½ by 10 ft (5 × 3 m), clinging by suction pads and tendrils. Leaves are bronzy dark green with silvery white veins, turning brilliant crimson before falling in autumn. Sun or light shade, best on north or east walls.

Photinia × fraseri 'Red Robin'　Brilliant red young foliage which matures to dark glossy green. Evergreen rounded bush up to 6½ ft (2 m) or more high, but can be pruned immediately after the leaves have matured to give a further flush of colour. Sun or light shade.

Pieris formosa 'Wakehurst'　Vivid red new leaves becoming dark green. When mature, erect or rounded evergreen shrub, 6 by 5 ft (1.8 × 1.5 m), with ivory-white flowers in April. Must have acid soil and shelter from late spring frosts, as growth starts early. Light shade. P. 'Forest Flame', similar with leaves turning through pink and creamy white as they age.

Pinus pumila 'Dwarf Blue'　Pine with long drooping blue-grey needles. Will form a flat-topped bush 1¼ by 1½ ft (0.4 × 0.5 m).

P. sylvestris 'Gold Coin'　Rounded bush reaching a maximum height of 3–6½ ft (1–2 m). Bluish needles turn bright golden during winter.

Rhamnus alaterna 'Argenteovariegata'　Develops into rounded bushy evergreen shrub, up to 8 ft (2.5 m) tall. Small glossy green leaves are mottled grey and margined with creamy white. Sun to deep shade.

Opposite: *Fothergilla major* has conspicuous flower spikes in spring, in addition to the beautifully coloured foliage in autumn

'Buttercup', the best yellow form of the common ivy, *Hedera helix*

Ribes sanguineum 'Brocklebankii' Flowering currant, 3 ft (1 m) tall and broad, with golden yellow leaves and pink flowers. Prune by removing three-year-old shoots after flowering. Light to moderate shade.

Salix lanata Willow with woolly, silvery green leaves, contrasting well with erect, yellowish grey catkins in spring. Makes low bush, 3 by 4 ft (1 × 1.2 m) Sun. Any moist soil.

Sambucus racemosa 'Plumosa Aurea' Deeply dissected, golden leaves and white flowers giving rise to red berries. Grows to 6½ by 5 ft (2 × 1.5 m) or more. Prune to restrain. Sun or light shade.

Weigela florida 'Variegata' Dense bush, 5 by 4 ft (1.5 × 1.2 m) with bright creamy white-margined leaves and pink flowers in June. Leave unpruned or remove three-year-old shoots after flowering. Sun or light shade.

W. praecox 'Variegata' Similar, with scented rose-pink flowers in May.

Plant Associations

The effectiveness of a particular plant is greatly enhanced if it is placed with an eye to the harmonizing colours or different foliage shapes of its neighbours, for example the silvery fern-like acaena combined with burgundy-coloured ajuga, or the reed-like foliage of miscantnus or yucca set off by the large rounded leaves of bergenia.

In the rock garden, shrub border or heather garden, the contrasting outline of a narrow upright conifer behind the low horizontal branches of junipers has a more lasting visual impact than any flower, which compensates to some extent for the lack of blossom and scent. On a larger scale, extravagantly weeping deciduous trees, such as *Betula pendula* 'Youngii' and *Prunus × yedoensis* 'Ivensii' (sometimes described as weeping like a crinoline), are seen at their best in winter and spring near the vertical columns of blue-grey conifers (see p. 246).

Some of the following suggestions for grouping plants include trees that can be planted sufficiently wide apart to make specimens, but close enough to be viewed in the same context, although this arrangement requires a fairly large amount of space. The trees have been chosen not for their flowers, which make a relatively brief contribution, but for the colours of their leaves, stems or barks.

Shrubs, perennials and grasses

Potentilla 'Elizabeth'; *Ceratostigma willmottianum*; and *Ruta graveolens* 'Jackman's Blue'. Colours: primrose yellow; and plumbago blue flowers; blue-grey foliage; late spring to early autumn.

Cotoneaster horizontalis; and *Euonymus fortunei* 'Silver Queen'. Colours: red berries; and creamy yellow variegated leaves; autumn and early winter (see p. 245).

Berberis thunbergii atropurpurea; and *Phlomis fruticosa*. Colours: purple foliage; and grey felted leaves with spikes of yellow flowers; summer.

Viburnum × bodnantense 'Dawn', with small spring bulbs. Colours: pink flowers; winter.

241

Cortaderia selloana 'Pumila'; and *Rhus typhina* 'Laciniata'. Colours: feathery silver plumes; and fern-like orange and yellow leaves; autumn.

Evergreen azaleas and rhododendrons with *Lilium hansonii*, *L. henryi*, *L. regale* and forms of *L. speciosum*. Colours: mixed; late spring to mid-summer.

Helictotrichon sempervirens with heathers. Colours: Glaucous-blue arching foliage and various flower and leaf colours; summer and winter.

Cornus alba 'Elegantissima'; and *Clematis* × *jackmanii*. Colours: greyish green leaves with silver edges; and blue flowers; summer.

Thuja occidentalis 'Rheingold'; and *Erica herbacea* 'King George'. Colours: rich old gold foliage; and rose pink flowers; winter.

Iris foetidissima; and *Bergenia cordifolia*. Colours: sword-like leaves with orange fruit; and large roundish deep green leaves; winter.

Corokia cotoneaster with ericas and callunas. Colours: small dainty leaves with yellow starry flowers and various; late spring, winter to summer for heathers.

Hydrangeas; and *Hemerocallis* 'Burning Daylight'. Colours: blue; and glowing orange flowers; summer to early autumn.

Hippophae rhamnoides; and *Cotinus coggygria* 'Royal Purple'. Colours: narrow silver leaves with orange berries; and deep purple leaves; summer and autumn.

Ceanothus 'Gloire de Versailles'; and various hemerocallis. Colours: blue; and pink, crimson or yellow flowers; mid-summer to autumn.

Cotinus coggygria 'Notcutt's Variety', *Cornus alba* 'Elegantissima', *Senecio* 'Sunshine', *Ceratostigma willmottianum* and floribunda roses 'Dearest' or 'Arthur Bell'. Colours: deep purple foliage, grey-green and cream variegated leaves combined with grey-felted leaves, blue flowers, salmon pink or yellow roses; from early summer to late autumn. Red bark and grey leaves in the winter.

Cortaderia selloana 'Pumila', *Kniphofia uvaria*, *Salvia officinalis* 'Purpurascens'. Colours: grey-green arching leaves, silvery grey plumes with coral spikes, soft purple foliage; from summer to late autumn.

Chamaecyparis lawsoniana 'Columnaris', *Hebe rakaiensis.*
Colours: glaucous blue and apple green leaves; all the year round.

Taxus baccata 'Standishii', *Lavandula spica* 'Hidcote'. Colours:
golden foliage, grey leaves and purple flowers from mid-summer
to autumn, evergreen foliage throughout the year.

Kniphofia 'Maid of Orleans', *Ceratostigma willmottianum,*
Anaphalis triplinervis, Hebe pinguifolia 'Pagei'. Colours: cream,
blue, white flowers, glaucous grey foliage; from early summer to
late autumn.

Fuchsia 'Mrs Popple', *Calluna vulgaris* 'Alba Plena', *Campanula*
portenschlagiana 'Major'. Colours: carmine and purple, white,
blue; from early summer to late autumn.

Potentilla fruticosa 'Elizabeth', *Nepeta* × *faassenii.* Colours:
primrose yellow, pastel-grey foliage, lavender blue flowers; from
early summer to late autumn.

Bergenia (all cultivars), hardy ferns, *Vinca major* 'Elegantissima'.
Colours: mainly foliage, large bottle green or reddish bronze
leaves, laciniate fronds, soft green edged with pale yellow
variegated leaves, blue; from spring to late autumn.

Cotinus coggygria 'Notcutt's Variety', *Hippophae rhamnoides.*
Colours: deep purple foliage, silver leaves, silver twigs, orange
berries; from early summer to late autumn.

Cotoneaster dammeri, Hebe albicans, H. rakaiensis, Ruta
graveolens 'Jackman's Blue'. Colours: deep green foliage, flowers
white, berries red, glaucous leaves, apple green leaves, opalescent
blue foliage.

Forsythia or *Chaenomeles, Pulmonaria angustifolia.* Colours:
yellow or pink and blue flowers; early spring.

Buddleja davidii cultivars, *Erica* and *Calluna.* Colours: purple,
pink; mid-summer to late autumn.

Rhododendron 'Britannia', *Saxifraga umbrosa.* Colours: ruby-red,
foamy pale pink inflorescence; late spring.

Floribunda rose 'Iceberg' or hybrid musk rose 'Prosperity',
Senecio cineraria 'White Diamond'. Colours: white, silver-grey
foliage with blue and mauve flowers; early summer to late
autumn.

Hamamelis mollis, Erica carnea. Colours: yellow, purplish pink;
mid-winter to early spring.

Corylus avellana 'Contorta', *Erica herbacea*. Colours: yellow catkins, twisted branches, purplish pink flowers; mid-winter to early spring.

Cotinus coggygria 'Notcutt's Variety', *Hedera colchica* 'Variegata'. Colours: deep purple foliage, blue-green, soft yellow variegated leaves.

Floribunda rose 'Iceberg', *Lavandula spica* 'Hidcote', *Agapanthus* Headbourne Hybrids, *Nepeta × faassenii*. Colours: white, grey leaves, purple flowers, blue and lavender blue flowers.

Cornus mas, *Muscari*, *Erica herbacea*. Colours: yellow, blue, purplish pink; mid-winter to early spring.

Phygelius capensis 'Coccineus', *Ceratostigma willmottianum*, *Senecio* 'Sunshine'. Colours: scarlet, plumbago-blue, felted grey leaves.

Trees

Pyrus salicifolia 'Pendula'; *Prunus spinosa* 'Purpurea'; and *Gleditsia triacanthos* 'Sunburst'. Colours: silver; deep purple; and gold foliage; summer.

Acer negundo 'Variegatum'; and *Prunus cerasifera* 'Pissardii'. Colours: leaves with irregular white margins; and dark red turning to purple; summer.

Acer platanoides 'Drummondii'; and *A. platanoides* 'Crimson King'. Colours: leaves with a marginal white band; and deep crimson-purple; summer.

Sorbus aria; and *Taxus baccata*. Colours: greyish green and white; and deep green leaves; summer.

Salix alba 'Sericea'; and *Corylus maxima* 'Purpurea'. Colours: bright silvery; and deep purple leaves; summer.

Betula pendula (deciduous); *Pinus sylvestris* (evergreen); and *Larix kaempferi* (deciduous). Colours: white stems; reddish young bark with blue-green leaves; and reddish purple twigs. Planted as a belt of trees, the silver birch, Scots pine and Japanese larch produce some of the most beautiful winter colour in the landscape.

Above: The rich autumn colour of *Cotoneaster horizontalis* (left) associates well with the variegated foliage of *Euonymus fortunei* 'Silver Queen' (right); both may be grown against a wall

Below: Daylilies like *Hemerocallis* 'Burning Daylight' (left) combine pleasantly with the popular *Ceanothus* 'Gloire de Versailles' (right)

Above: *Staphylea holocarpa*, the bladder nut, may be grown as a tree or large shrub
Below: The contrasting shapes and colours of *Betula pendula* 'Youngii' and conifers, illustrated on a small scale

Scent in the Garden

While a camellia or a nerine is bound to be admired for its elegance or beauty, even the most demure and humble flower is cherished if it can offer scent. Mignonette and lily-of-the-valley, for example, would probably not receive a second glance were it not for the fragrance of their flowers. There are many more scented plants than can be mentioned here, but my purpose is to select a few shrubs that are valuable for their perfume, most of them deservedly popular for this very reason.

Many of the shrubs which are appreciated for winter-flowering have the bonus of fragrant blossom. This certainly applies to *Viburnum* x *bodnantense* 'Dawn', which bears sprays of richly scented pink flowers from November until February, interrupted only by the severest weather. The Chinese witch-hazel, *Hamamelis mollis*, has already been recommended (see p. 108). Its delicious perfume on one of those fleeting but precious sunny days we sometimes experience in January helps to make up for the bleakness of winter and the clusters of golden yellow strap-like flowers seem oblivious to frost and snow. The fragrant parchment-like blooms of the winter sweet, *Chimonanthus praecox*, pale yellow stained purple at the centre, are a joy to see in December and January, although this shrub is relatively uncommon, perhaps because it does not flower until it is established. The cultivar 'Luteus' has slightly larger flowers of a uniform waxy yellow, opening a little later, but is equally fragrant.

A shrubby honeysuckle, *Lonicera* x *purpusii*, contributes winter blossom and scent with freely borne creamy white flowers in January and February. It can be trained against a low wall so that the perfume may be savoured near the house. The sarcococcas are useful low-growing evergreens, with small white flowers opening in late winter. Though modest, these are scented and the bluish green willow-like foliage combines well with paving and stone. They will grow in shady places that are not too dry and *S.humilis* makes good ground cover.

As spring approaches, *Mahonia japonica* offers some of the best scented blossom of the year, producing clusters of lemon-coloured flowers in long racemes from February to early March above bold, leathery, soft green foliage. Properly placed, it is a fine feature, but lacks the imposing upright habit of other mahonias which are so useful in garden design. At the same time of year, the exquisite perfume of *Daphne mezereum* cannot be ignored and

the clustered, wax-like, reddish purple flowers on leafless stems are a beautiful sight, particularly when seen above a blanket of pure white snow, which is not an unusual occurrence in March. Other daphnes, *D*. 'Somerset', *D. collina* and *D. retusa*, make their presence equally known in May, with blooms in shades of pink and purple. One of the most powerfully fragrant shrubs is *Viburnum* × *juddii*, which is in full blossom at the end of April with rounded heads of white-flushed pink flowers.

The garden would seem incomplete without the perfume of the lilac. The many cultivars of *Syringa vulgaris*, ranging in colour from white to red, blue or purple, are a delight from May into June. Azaleas, rhododendrons and tree heaths, with their heady scent from April to June, would be an important part of a scented garden, although it must be remembered that these require acid soils.

The mock orange is reminiscent of long warm days in June, when its fragrance mingles with the smells of a summer garden. Two hybrids of moderate size suitable for a smaller garden are *Philadelphus* 'Beauclerk' and *P*. 'Silver Showers'. The Mount Etna broom, *Genista aetnensis*, is a graceful shrub with golden yellow scented flowers on almost leafless thread-like branches in July. In planting schemes it provides a light and airy tallness up to 18 feet (5.4 m) high without casting shade. The Spanish broom, *Spartium junceum*, is closely related but more bushy and twiggy. Unlike most brooms, it holds its very fragrant flowers over a long period, from June to September.

Above: *Hamamelis mollis*, one of the most valuable winter-flowering shrubs, bearing fragrant blooms from December to March
Below: The charming mezereon, *Daphne mezereum*, a small deciduous shrub which flourishes on chalky soils
Overleaf: The richly tinted autumn leaves of *Fothergilla major* are preceded by bottle-brush flowers in late spring

Index

Page numbers in **bold** type refer to illustrations